**Community Care
Practice Handbooks**

General Editor: Martin Davies

Working With Drug Users

Community Care
Practice Handbooks

General Editor: Martin Davies

Working With Drug Users

Ronno Griffiths
Brian Pearson

COMMUNITY
CARE
THE INDEPENDENT VOICE OF SOCIAL WORK

Wildwood
House

Published by
Wildwood House
Gower House
Croft Road
Aldershot
Hants GU11 3HR
England

Distributed in the United States by
Gower Publishing Comapny
Old Post Road
Brookfield
Vermont 05036
USA

British Library Cataloguing in Publication Data

Griffiths, Ronno
   Working with drug users. — (Community care
   practice handbooks; 25).
   1. Drug abuse — Great Britain — Prevention
   2. Drug abuse —Treatment — Great Britain
   I. Title II. Pearson, Brian III. Series
   362.2 ' 93 ' 0941   HV5840.G7

ISBN 0 7045 0582 7

Printed and bound in Great Britain by
Biddles Limited, Guildford and King's Lynn

Contents

1 The Current Situation

> We see this [drug abuse] as the most serious peacetime threat to our national well being. (House of Commons Select Committee on Home Affairs, 1985)

The Select Committee's words articulate a widespread concern that a vast and nameless threat hangs over the future of our culture. They are also, many would argue, deeply misleading. To set them in perspective, we need to look at the changing pattern of socially-disapproved drug use over the last two decades.

The use of opiate-based preparations was a commonplace and little re-marked feature of nineteenth-century life (Berridge and Edwards 1981), but for the greater part of the present century Britain has been an under-using society when it comes to drugs. It was not until the 1960s that widespread public concern arose over the use of psychoactive substances. Nevertheless, earlier in the century, largely under American pressure, the UK had been signatory to an international convention designed to control drug use and availability and had enacted corresponding domestic legislation in the Dangerous Drugs Act 1920 (Jamieson, Glanz and MacGregor 1984). In 1926, the Rolleston Committee laid down guidelines for the treatment of opiate dependence which were to remain the basis of our response until well into the 1980s. The so-called 'British system', which has been criticized as neither British nor systematic, kept open the possibility of treating opiate misuse as a medical problem and so helped to avoid the worst excesses of the American response which handled opiate use solely by means of criminal sanctions. Doctors, the Committee felt, were justified in prescribing opiates to addicts:

(a) when undergoing treatment for the cure of addiction by the gradual withdrawal method;
(b) when, after every effort had been made to overcome addiction, the drug could not be withdrawn completely, either because withdrawal produced symptoms which could not be treated satisfactorily under the conditions of private practice (i.e. other than in a hospital); or because the patient, while capable of leading a useful and fairly normal life so long as he took a certain non-progressive quantity, usually small, of the drug of addiction, ceased to be able to do so when the regular allowance is withdrawn. (Rolleston Committee 1926)

Throughout the first half of the century, this system functioned reasonably well. The number of known opiate users (and most of them were known) remained stable at around 400-500. They were predominantly middle-aged and middle-class. Over half were women. Many had become dependent as the result of medical treatment. Many others were doctors, nurses, or others with easy professional access to drugs. In no sense did these people constitute a cohesive sub-culture. Their troubles were private, a matter between their doctors, their immediate families and themselves. Many continued to hold down responsible jobs and to function well in society.

In 1961, a committee under the chairmanship of Lord Brain reported that the situation had not changed noticeably over the years and that the recommendations of the Rolleston Committee needed no revision. Almost immediately afterwards, as if to mock their efforts, disturbing reports began to circulate of a dramatic upsurge in drug use. Lord Brain's committee was hastily reconvened and in 1965 published a second report painting a much more worrying picture.

A new generation of opiate users had begun to emerge, who differed markedly from their respectable predecessors. Predominantly young males, often socially marginal, they formed a relatively cohesive sub-culture, saw heroin as a valued component of their life-style and had a tendency to proselytize, to 'turn on' their friends and acquaintances. At much the same time, the use of other drugs — cannabis, the amphetamines, etc., began to increase in popularity. The youth culture of the 'swinging sixties' had begun its well-publicized march to notoriety.

The second Brain Committee's findings were influential and all but one of its recommendations resulted in government action, the exception being its suggestion that treatment be made compulsory. The response and pattern of service delivery during the 1970s owes much, for good or ill, to the committee's labours.

Concerned by what it saw as the role which over-prescribing by a 'handful of doctors' had played in escalating the use of heroin, the committee proposed that the power to prescribe heroin and cocaine for the purpose of treating addiction should be removed from the generality of doctors and confined to specially licensed members of the profession. This proposal led to the setting up of a number of specialist drug treatment clinics within the NHS, headed by consultant psychiatrists and charged with the task of attracting and treating all those dependent on opiates. Additionally, it was hoped that by judiciously adjusting the level of prescribing, the clinics would be able to prevent the establishment of an organized criminal black market in the opiates of the kind which existed in the United States. Drug misuse became a medical speciality, and the doctor's primary responsibility to the welfare of the individual patient became dangerously complicated by the addition of what could be interpreted as either a public health or a policing function. But the system still allowed the opiate user to be treated as a person in need of medical help and retained the Rolleston Committee's view that to prescribe opiates could be a legitimate form of treatment.

This complication in the doctor's role reflected a contradiction in the British approach to drug misuse which the Brain Committee did nothing to resolve. Should drug takers be seen as suffering from an illness and as therefore not responsible for their drug-related behaviour, or should they be looked upon as criminals and so accountable for their law-breaking? The addict, according to Brain, was a 'sick person, provided he does not resort to criminal acts' when, as Peter Laurie wryly commented 'presumably, he is no longer sick' (Laurie 1971). The sick/criminal dichotomy is seen on the individual level in many drug users' tendency to oscillate between doctor and prison, and institutionally in the division of responsibility for drug misuse between the Home Office and the Department of Health and Social Security. Penal and treatment responses to drugs have marched hand in hand.

In 1971, as the climax to a minor flurry of drugs legislation, parliament passed the Misuse of Drugs Act, which laid down penalties for the possession, supply, import, export and manufacture of a very wide range of substances. The act categorized drugs into classes, A, B and C according to what was seen as their potential for harm, with offences involving Class A drugs attracting the highest penalties and those involving Class C drugs the lowest. In addition, and again following the Brain Committee's recommendations, it imposed a statutory responsibility upon doctors attending anyone whom they considered, or had reasonable grounds to suspect, to be dependent upon any notifiable drug to report that fact to the Chief Medical Officer at the Home Office. 'Notifiable drugs' are: cocaine, heroin, morphine, methadone (Physeptone), dipipanone (Diconal), dextromoramide (Palfium), hydrocodone, hydromorphone, levorphanol, oxycodone, pethidine, phenazocine, piritramide and opium. With the exception of cocaine, these are all opiate-like drugs: there is no obligation for doctors to notify those dependent upon any other drug.

At about the same time as the drug dependence clinics were being established, a number of residential and non-residential facilities were set up by voluntary bodies, quickly built up considerable expertise and formed a valuable addition to service provision. Unlike the clinics, which were designed to deal almost exclusively with those dependent upon the opiates, these non-statutory bodies made no exclusions on any drugs their clientele might be using. A small number of 'street agencies', providing counselling, advice, information and referral services, came into being, aiming to reduce the harm which their clients experienced through their drug-taking and to assist them to stabilize their drug use and eventually stop altogether. Non-statutory bodies also became the main supplier of residential services, particularly of residential rehabilitation for those unable to maintain a drug-free state while still living in their community. Outside of the NHS drug clinics, virtually all specialist services for drug users were provided by non-statutory bodies until well into the 1980s and their role remains crucial as the chief source of non-medical expertise and experience.

Over the years, drug clinics have successively modified their treatment response, moving quickly away from prescribing heroin, substituting for it first injectable methadone (a synthetic opiate) and then oral preparations of the same drug. At the same time, most have become increasingly unwilling to countenance long-term maintenance prescribing of any opiate. The Advisory Council on the Misuse of Drugs (ACMD 1982), while finding itself unable to come down firmly on either side of the debate, at least implicitly welcomed this trend. New clinic patients are likely to be offered only a short-term reducing prescription of oral methadone, although many older patients still continue to be maintained. However, clinics are far from unanimous in their attitudes, and policies vary quite widely.

Throughout the period, the number of opiate dependants coming to the notice of the Home Office continued to increase at an average rate of 9% a year. But after the panic of the 1960s, for most of the 1970s public and politicians sank back into a comfortable conviction that drug use had gone away. In fact nothing of the sort had occurred: it had merely become less visible. Media interest waned and for ten years there was no debate on drugs in either house of parliament.

Statistics in this area are notoriously incomplete. All of the figures which are routinely collected present at best a biased and partial picture of the actual situation. Nevertheless, despite their shortcomings, official statistics can be useful in displaying trends, even if they fall far short of a complete enumeration of the real population of drug users.

Home Office notifications of opiate dependants

Under the terms of the Misuse of Drugs Act, doctors who in the course of their work attend anyone whom they know or suspect to be dependent upon any of fourteen specified drugs (opiates, plus cocaine) have a statutory duty to report such patients to the Home Office. Every year, the Home Office publishes the aggregate figures, together with the figures of drug seizures and of offences under the Misuse of Drugs Act.

Throughout the 1970s, the notification figures sustained a steady, if unspectacular, upward trend, a trend unnoticed by politicians, media and the public, all apparently comfortably convinced that drug misuse had been a short-lived aberration of the 1960s. Drugs workers, who throughout most of the decade had composed their jeremiads of impending doom unheard, found themselves, perhaps rather to their own secret surprise, vindicated when the 1980s saw a dramatic rise in the reported incidence of heroin misuse. Between 1980 and 1983, the number of notified addicts (the vast majority to heroin) doubled (see Table 1.1).

Table 1.1 Numbers of addicts known to the Home Office 1975-1985

1975	1976	1977	1978	1979	1980	1981	1982	1983	1984	1985
3425	3474	3605	4116	4787	5107	6157	7962	10,235	12,489	14,688

Source: derived from Home Office (1986).

The average age of new addicts in 1984 was 26, a figure which had remained stable for decades. In 1985 it dropped to 25. Between 1979 and that year, there was a notable increase in the proportion of first-time notifications aged under 21, who in 1985 constituted 24% of the total. Since research indicates that individuals tend to use for a number of years before being notified, this suggests that considerable numbers of adolescents are now using opiates. Just over 70% of new notifications were male, a slight decline from the figure of 75% during the 1970s. In 1985, 92% of new addicts were described as addicted to heroin, as compared with 76% in1982 and about 60% in 1978.

The publication of two influential reports by the Advisory Council on the Misuse of Drugs (ACMD 1982 and 1984) coincided with rising public concern, amounting at times to panic, at what was seen as an epidemic of drug use. The Government responded by establishing a DHSS central funding initiative to pump-prime local projects in England. Similar funding arrangements were made for Scotland and Wales. In June 1984, the DHSS issued Circular HC(84)14/LAC(84)12 which required English health authorities to take early action to improve services for drug users and to report back on their plans. The circular stated that ministers attached the highest priority to the improvement of services for drug users. The Welsh Office and the Scottish Home and Health Department took action along the same lines. A number of new services, both within and without the NHS, were established and some existing facilities were able to expand their resources. From 1986, a further £5 million a year was made available for the expansion of services. By early 1986, £13.4 million had been allocated under the Central Funding Initiative to 162 new or existing projects in England and corresponding arrangements were underway in Scotland and Wales. Many health authorities have used this money to set up community-based services, often staffed by social workers and community psychiatric nurses. The scale of the increase in service provision has been remarkable when it is remembered that in 1981 there were only 25 non-hospital based services for drug users employing paid staff and 16 purely volunteer groups in England and Wales and none at all in Scotland (ACMD 1982). It is doubtful, however if supply has yet caught up with demand and the distribution and coordination of services remains highly variable.

An interdepartmental Ministerial Group on the Misuse of Drugs was established in 1984, to coordinate and develop the government's response to the rise in drug use, envisaged as a five-pronged attack designed to reduce supplies from abroad; make enforcement more effective; strengthen deterrence and tighten domestic controls; develop prevention; and improve treatment and rehabilitation (Home Office 1986a).

Other indicators confirm an upward trend in the use of drugs and draw attention to substances not covered by the notification figures. It is worth stressing this point, since there is a strong tendency to concentrate just on heroin and to ignore other drugs. Note particularly the rise in convictions for amphetamines shown in Table 1.2.

Table 1.2 Persons found guilty or cautioned for drug offences, by type of drug

Type of drug	1979	1980	1981	1982	1983	1984	1985
Cocaine	331	476	566	426	563	698	631
Heroin	520	751	808	966	1,508	2,446	3,226
Methadone	298	363	445	404	379	411	413
Dipipanone	453	440	498	566	370	252	97
LSD	208	246	345	466	451	558	539
Cannabis	12,409	14,910	15,388	17,410	19,966	20,529	20,976
Amphetamines	760	827	1,074	1,521	2,008	2,501	2,946
Other drugs	1,165	1,292	1,141	1,008	946	975	1,023
All drugs	14,339	17,158	17,921	20,319	23,341	25,022	26,596

Source: Home Office (1986b).

Table 1.3 shows drugs seizures by Customs and Excise and the police. Once again the rise in heroin is unmistakable. The bulk of drugs are seized by customs officers, rather than by the police and Customs refuses to speculate what percentage of the total coming into the country it manages to intercept, although the figure of approximately 15% is often quoted. These figures reflect a significant change in the pattern of drug supply.

Table 1.3 Seizures of heroin, cocaine and amphetamines (in kilogrammes)

	1979	1980	1981	1982	1983	1984	1985
Heroin	44.9	38.2	93.4	195.5	236.2	361.6	366.4
Cocaine	24.0	40.2	21.1	18.8	80.0	65.5	85.4
Amphetamines	8.6	5.2	18.1	13.6	34.9	58.8	76.6

Source: Home Office (1986b).

Throughout the 1960s and 1970s, the illicit drug market in opiates was largely fuelled by diversion of pharmaceutical products, for instance by addicts selling part of their prescriptions, by break-ins to pharmacies, or by thefts from pharmaceutical warehouses. The present decade has seen the establishment of fairly large-scale importation of illegal drugs, in the case of heroin and cocaine, or of illegal manufacture, mostly home-based, in the case of amphetamines. The cannabis market, once dominated by amateur enthusiasts, is now the domain of organized crime. These changes have profound implications for control and prevention strategies.

The government has reacted by committing (rather minimal) funds to help international efforts to control drug supply; by increasing Customs and Excise staff specifically concerned with combatting drug smuggling; by forming a new police National Drugs Intelligence Unit; and by the establishment of a drug squad in all police forces. A number of new substances, including the barbiturates and benzodiazepines, have been brought under the control of the Misuse of Drugs Act. In addition, doctors now require a special licence to prescribe dipipanone for the treatment of addiction. The penalty for trafficking in Class A drugs has been increased to life imprisonment, and parole restricted for traffickers sentenced to more than five years imprisonment. The Drug Trafficking (Offences) Act 1986 allows for the confiscation of assets of those convicted of trafficking in drugs. Concern about solvent abuse ensured the passage of the Intoxicating Substances (Supply) Act 1985, which makes it an offence to supply solvents to a person under 18 if it is known or suspected that the solvent will be used for the purpose of causing intoxication.

In the domain of prevention, somewhat controversial poster and television campaigns were launched in 1985. Leaflets and booklets designed to inform parents and professionals of the issues were disseminated; video packages designed for use with professionals and with young people were produced; and the Department of Education and Science made £2 million available to fund drug education posts.

The effect on treatment services of changes in drug availability is of great importance, for the supply of opiates has become almost completely independent of the NHS. This has two major results. First, while opiate users' supplies are secure and while they can afford to pay for them, they are unlikely to seek medical attention of their own accord. The same argument applies to cocaine and amphetamine use. Second, the increased availability consequent to the organization of the drugs trade means that far greater numbers are likely to become involved in problematic drug use. When these users do eventually get round to seeking help, they are likely to find it spread very thinly on the ground, since although new specialist services have been set up, such provision has not kept pace with the increase in use. Services are increasingly becoming overburdened, and long waiting lists for an appointment at a drug clinic, for example, are the rule rather than the exception. Thus entry into drug use becomes easier and escape from it more difficult.

Our ability to know how many opiate users there are is also diminished. The Home Office notification figures rely on doctors' willingness to inform the Home Office of their drug-dependent patients, and also on the motivation of drug users to approach doctors, one source of motivation being the hope of obtaining drugs. In the past, when drug supplies were significantly dependent on doctors' willingness to prescribe, the notification figures were probably a reasonably accurate indicator of actual numbers of drug users. But this is no longer the case, as the Home Office is the first to admit. It is generally believed that nowadays notifications underestimate the true incidence by a factor of about five.

Research in London by the Drug Indicators Project (Hartnoll and Grey 1986) concludes that the total number of people using opiates regularly (defined as daily or almost daily use for at least four consecutive weeks) at some time during 1984 totalled between 20,000 and 30,000, about 1% of the population aged 16 to 44 years, and that the number of occasional users exceeds that of the regulars. The research suggested that, of regular opiate users

perhaps no more than one in ten are under the age of 20. The majority, around two thirds, are in their twenties, but a significant proportion, about one quarter are in their 30's. About one third are female. There is no 'typical' social background, nor are there clear factors which distinguish people who use from those who do not. About three quarters are unemployed. Traditionally, the various ethnic minorities have been underrepresented amongst opioid users [i.e. users of opiates and related drugs]. There are now indications that this is changing.

It appears that there are three broad 'generations' of opioid users.

(1) An ageing cohort of long term addicts from the 1960s/70s who were adolescents when they first started and are now in their 30s.

(2) People who had long experience of using a variety of other drugs (ampheta-

mines, cannabis, LSD, etc) who did not start to use heroin until the late 1970s/ early 1980s when they were already in their late 20s or early 30s. In many cases, they sniffed heroin rather than injected it. (3) young people in their late teens or early 20s who started to use heroin in the early 1980s, a year or two after the older group of initiates. They were more likely to smoke heroin and to live in working class areas.

In a working-class area of south London, it was found (Griffiths and Barker 1984) that heroin users included, in addition to a few traditional long-term addicts, a group of young users of both sexes, ranging in age from 14 years to the early twenties; a group of users in their early twenties, whose lives seemed despairing and without apparent direction; a group of older working-class men who had been and to some extent still were heavily involved in traditional drinking patterns; and a group of young mothers in their early twenties. About 40% of heroin users were young women.

Despite official denials, there is evidence in a number of recent studies of a correlation between unemployment, social deprivation and heroin use. Research in Glasgow (Haw 1985), the Wirral (Parker *et al.* 1986) and in the north of England (Pearson *et al.* 1987) all point to this conclusion.

In the country as a whole, a conservative estimate would put the number of regular heroin users at some 60,000. Amphetamine use is probably even more prevalent and cocaine is widely available. LSD has become more popular once again and cannabis continues to be by far the most widely practised form of 'illegal' drug use. Solvent abuse, despite its media eclipse by heroin, is still widespread. Problems stemming from the use of prescription drugs (notably the benzodiazepines with an estimate of a quarter of a million users experiencing difficulties), tobacco and alcohol undoubtedly outstrip those associated with more stigmatized forms of drug use, but evoke comparatively little public concern.

Finally, an entirely new dimension has been added by the current concern about the spread of Acquired Immune Deficiency Syndrome (AIDS). Injecting drug users and their sexual contacts are at high risk of infection by the HIV virus and of subsequently developing AIDS. Much thought is being given both to ways of limiting the spread of infection and to providing services to support those drug users who are antibody positive or who develop the syndrome itself.

2 Stereotypes and Attitudes

A custome lothsome to the eye, hatefull to the nose, harmefull to the brain, dangerous to the lungs, and in the black stinking fume thereof, nearest resembling the horrible Stigian smoke of the pit that is bottomlesse. (James I. *Counterblaste to Tobacco*, 1604)

Reality is for people who can't handle drugs. (Contemporary slogan)

There is almost no human society that has not made use of chemical substances to alter states of consciousness (Weil 1972). Equally universally, all societies have strong beliefs about precisely which substances can be employed to this end and about the circumstances in which their use is legitimate.

'Drug' in the context of phrases like 'drug problem' or 'drug abuse' is really shorthand for 'socially disapproved drug' or 'drug which is used in socially disapproved ways'. The strength of that social disapproval can be startling and remarkably resistant to rational argument. If patterns of drug-taking have changed markedly in the last two decades, public attitudes have shown no corresponding shift.

The terrifying growth in drug abuse on a world scale will lead ultimately to civilisation being destroyed, Leighton-Linslade's Euro MP Peter Beazley has warned. Effective steps must be taken now by the nations of the world to crush this scourge of mankind, he said. (*Beds. and Bucks. Observer*, 28 October 1986)

If such attitudes were based upon an accurate assessment of a substance's potential for harm to the individual or to society, things would be well enough, but this is seldom so. The public perception of a drug's harmfulness depends upon many factors, of which the actual pharmacological effects are often the least important.

Factors which influence social attitudes to drugs

1. The source from which the drug is obtained
Drugs obtained from a doctor and used under the auspices of medical treatment are likely to be seen as less dangerous and more socially acceptable than would otherwise be the case. Methadone is a case in point. The prescribed use of this synthetic opiate in the treatment of heroin dependence

would be looked upon with considerably more favour by most people than would the use for hedonistic purposes of the same drug bought on the street. The high status of the medical profession confers legitimacy on whatever doctors choose to prescribe. One exception to this generalization is the growing disquiet in recent years about the use of the minor tranquillizers, which has come about because of increased public awareness of the possible dangers of this class of drugs, and marches in step with worries about orthodox medicine as a whole.

2. The drug's legal status

The fact that a drug is subject to stringent legal controls will lead to negative attitudes towards its use, presumably because there is a tendency to assume that if a substance is so controlled, then this in itself is good evidence of its potential for harm. This superficially reasonable assumption ignores the complex process by which a substance may find itself included, say, within the provisions of the Misuse of Drugs Act. If proven potential for harm was the principal or only reason for inclusion, then tobacco and alcohol would be much more severely controlled than they are.

> Deaths caused directly by illicit drugs (235 in 1984) are but a fraction of deaths caused by tobacco (100,000 a year) or alcohol (5,000-8,000). ... Tobacco and alcohol related diseases are susceptible to prevention, yet the government does little. Illicit drugs by definition, do not benefit the government, but taxes on alcohol raise revenue of £6,000 million a year, and tobacco over £4,000 million. (AAA 1986).

3. Public familiarity with the drug's effects

Within limits, the more familiar we are with a drug's mood altering effects, the more sanguine we are likely to be about its use. This is best illustrated by the case of alcohol. In the United Kingdom, alcohol is widely used: it is calculated that not more than 5% of men and 12% of women are totally abstinent (Dight 1976). As a result, British society has a detailed body of folk knowledge about alcohol, and elaborate sets of social rules for regulating its consumption. Most importantly, we have available to us social concepts such as 'acceptable drinking' and 'problem drinking' and are sure, most of the time, that we can distinguish between them. So, although we are aware of the physical and social harm that can arise from overindulgence and although we may invoke legal sanctions against drunken behaviour that inconveniences or endangers others, there is no strong body of opinion in this country calling for the prohibition of alcohol and for the imprisonment of brewers and distillers as 'merchants of death'. Contrast this with the position of heroin. Most of us have no personal knowledge of the effects of this drug against which to evaluate the wilder claims about its destructive powers and so are likely to accept them at face value and react accordingly. Unlike alcohol, there is no socially available category of 'acceptable heroin use': most people would find the phrase meaningless and perverse. All heroin use (except possibly for the relief of terminal pain) is seen, by default, as unacceptable, and as leading inevitably to addiction, degradation and death.

4. *Our familiarity with users*

We fear what we do not know. Thus, the less we know about the true effects of drugs and the less we come into contact with drug users, the easier it is to project fantasies on to them. This happens even more readily if the users are thought to be members of a group which is socially marginal or already the object of disquiet. Drug use is associated with young people in the public mind, and the younger generation is notoriously prone to be labelled as troublesome by its elders. It is interesting to speculate what might have happened if LSD, when its use was still legal, had first become popular among cabinet ministers and captains of industry, rather than among the youth 'counter-culture'. To some extent, drugs are damned by association with the already stigmatized groups by which they are thought, correctly or otherwise, to be used. Their use of drugs then becomes another reason for further stigmatizing the group, thus completing the circle. An example of this process at work can be seen in the way in which cocaine use became criminalized in the United States at the beginning of this century. Musto (1973) argues that the desire of southern politicians to repress the black population lay behind the campaign to change the law. Cocaine use was first associated in the public mind with blacks, who were then alleged to commit appalling crimes (notably against white women) while under its influence. New laws against cocaine were introduced and its use by blacks was then employed to legitimate further measures against the black community, including its disenfranchisement. In this country, marijuana use is often popularly associated with young blacks – although in reality whites are rather more likely to have used it than are blacks – and this connection serves both to harden attitudes towards the drug and to justify repressive policing methods against black youth.

5. *The reasons why the drug is believed to be used*

If a drug is believed to be used for the relief of some distress, physical or psychological, its use will be less disapproved than if the reason for use is seen as basically hedonistic, or self-indulgent. This may be part of the reason why those dependent on minor tranquillizers are pitied, rather than condemned. Heroin use, on the other hand, is seen as hedonistic. Young (1971) has postulated that drug users are resented for obtaining 'unearned pleasure' through their use of drugs, contrary to the protestant ethic which holds that pleasures have to be the result of hard work. In compensation, they have to be seen as suffering unimaginable torments in the end. The relish that the media take in recounting the horrors of withdrawal from heroin lends some support to this thesis.

6. *Cultural factors*

The way in which attitudes vary from culture to culture and over time, points out more clearly than anything else the relative unimportance of pharmacological effects as such (as against what they are *believed* to be) in determining responses to drugs. In contrast to western tolerance of alcohol consumption, Islamic societies may strongly penalize its use (as unfortunate expatriates in Saudi Arabia have occasionally discovered to their cost) whilst at the same time taking a far more relaxed view of cannabis. A few years ago, Colonel Zia outlawed the traditional use of opium in Pakistan, incidentally encouraging a flourishing heroin trade to the West by so doing. Tobacco provides an instructive case of changing social perceptions of a drug, from James the First and Sixth's impassioned tirade against tobacco, through the apogee of its acceptability in the middle years of this century, to its present descent into disgrace as its adverse health effects have become better known. Coffee was once disapproved of because of its association with the political subversives who frequented eighteenth-century coffee houses, and the recent minor flood of research on the ill-effects of caffeine shows signs of further tarnishing its image amongst health-conscious sections of the community. There was a time in the early nineteenth century when pundits seriously prophesied the ruin of the English labouring man as a result of his newly acquired taste for tea in preference to the beer which had sustained him in former, less degenerate times. Later in the century, the temperance movement had reversed this stand, intemperately praising the cup that cheers, but does not inebriate. In the United States, until well into this century, heroin was freely available over the counter and was marketed as a sovereign specific for a wide range of ailments in very much the way that aspirin is today. Legal changes almost overnight transformed the image of the heroin taker from that of an ordinary member of society to that of a desperate and criminal deviant. The properties of the drug presumably remained the same.

These factors interact in complicated ways to affect public attitudes. What is believed about a drug is considerably more important in terms of social consequences than whether or not that belief is factually correct. People may not be in a position to determine the truth, or not bother to find out, or may even actively resist enlightment, to the discomfiture of self-proclaimed experts.

That attitudes to drug use are so strongly held and often so tenuously tied to facts should be a matter of no small concern. How drugs are seen has an important bearing on how drug takers are perceived. Negative and ill-formed beliefs about drugs can be expected to translate themselves into negative and ill-judged reactions to users. The implications for policy formation, legislation, investment in services, the willingness of professionals to involve themselves in work with drug users and, not least, the self-image of users and their experience of the world, are profound. Schur (1964) discusses the ways in which social reactions mould and even create certain problematic features of drug use.

> Certain aspects of addict behaviour (notably addict-crime, involvement in trafficking, development of addict-subculture) cannot directly be attributed either to the effects of drugs or to psychological characteristics of the individuals involved. Rather the presence or absence of such behaviour appears to be determined largely by the nature of the societal reaction to the addict.

One cannot overstress the importance of workers being clear about their own attitudes to drugs and drug users and of basing these attitudes on an informed and dispassionate consideration of the facts. They will crucially affect every interaction with drug-using clients, at the extreme even dictating whether the worker sees the client's drug use as problematic or not, irrespective of actual circumstances. In a host of more subtle ways they will colour the therapeutic relationship, helping or hampering the establishment of trust. Problems may also arise in dealing with the parents or relatives of drug users, whose own attitudes may be at odds in different ways with those of both the drug user and the worker. Difficulties can also be encountered with colleagues or with other agencies, where their attitudes and opinions on the best way of handling a case differ from one's own. In all such situations, clarity about one's own position and the reasons for it will work for the benefit of the client.

All too often, a term like 'drug taker' or 'addict' functions as a 'master status', as a title which is assumed to tell us all we need to know about someone and which entitles us to apply a stereotyped list of additional attributes to that person. A group of social workers asked to brainstorm words which they felt were commonly evoked by the description 'drug taker', produced the following list.

young	punk	frightened
male	self-indulgent	dangerous
depressed	drop-outs	unemployed
dirty	victims	inadequate
hippy	criminal	amoral
irresponsible	doomed	working-class
sick	pushers	manipulative
self-destructive	aggressive	rich kids

What is at stake here is not whether it is possible to find some drug takers who conform to many of these stereotypes (it certainly is), but the effects of such widespread negative labelling on public reactions to drug use. The common tendency to see users as 'undeserving', as suffering from wilfully self-inflicted and peculiarly intractable injuries, has seriously handicapped the development of social policy in this area. Until recently, drug users have come very far down anyone's list of funding priorities. As a result, those seeking help with their problems have often failed to find it. Such stereotyping has mystified drug use, frightening off and deskilling workers who find themselves faced with a drug-using client, and perhaps causing them to miss the possible contribution of drug use to clients' problems where the client does not fit the workers' stereotypes of a drug taker. That most workers receive little or no input on drug use in the course of their professional training exacerbates this reaction. The handling of 'drug abuse' has become ghettoized, conceived as the domain of specialists, armed with arcane knowledge and skills not available to the ordinary worker in the helping professions.

This is doubly unfortunate. Given the present rate of increase in problem drug use, existing specialist services are under severe strain and cannot hope to cope with the potential demand on their resources. The economic climate makes it inconceivable that sufficient funding will be made available to create enough new services to cope adequately with the spiralling number of users. If users are to receive help, it is imperative for generic services to become involved. Even if this were not the case, it is surely desirable that drug users do not remain cut off from the resources of services to which most other sections of the community have access. Such isolation can only serve to perpetuate the unnecessary degree of public fear and hostility which surrounds them and hamper their efforts to deal with their problems. Clients who make the conscious decision to approach a specialist drug service typically only do so at a relatively late stage in their drug-using careers, when they themselves have recognized the existence of a drug-related problem which they can no longer ignore. This limits the ability of specialist services to engage in early intervention, before such problems have become fully manifest. The Advisory Council on the Misuse of Drugs (ACMD 1982) concluded:

we have proposed a problem oriented approach which recognises that the drug misuser may experience a range of problems and that drug misuse is just one factor. We are concerned that the majority of specialist services are designed for those who are most seriously affected by their drug misuse and who consequently have multiple problems, whilst limited services are available for those whose drug misuse often debars them from non-specialist services yet makes them inappropriate for specialist services.

The inclusion of non-specialist services in the range of available provision is, in our opinion, essential if specific problems are to be dealt with at an early stage, thus limiting potential damage to the individual. The services which we identify as having a valuable role to play include primary medical services, social services departments, the probation and after-care service (social work departments in Scotland), housing departments and housing associations, employment services (including any special provisions for training and work experience). Non-specialist services also have an important role to play in providing aspects of a treatment package within a perspective of rehabilitation.

While there will always be a place for specialist agencies, it is essential that generic services become more involved. The skills needed to deal competently with clients' drug-related problems are precisely the professional skills already possessed by social workers and those in allied professions. In undertaking this task, workers may have to grapple, not only with their own attitudes and those of the drug user's family and community, but also the possibly discrepant attitudes of other workers and services with an interest in the client's welfare. It is the purpose of this book to provide a modicum of necessary specialist knowledge and to try to show how existing skills can be applied to work with drug users.

3 Some Definitions and General Hazards

Professionals often confess that ignorance of drugs and their effects contributes to their unhappiness about working with drug users. It is true that to cope effectively with drug-using clients, one needs to be broadly familiar with the effects of different classes of drugs. However, this does not mean that it is necessary to commit to memory the entire contents of the British Pharmacopeia. This and the following chapter aim to equip workers with sufficient knowledge of drugs, their effects, and the possible hazards associated with their use, in order to be able to respond intelligently to the drug-using client.

The World Health Organization (WHO 1970) defined drug dependency as:

> A state, psychic and sometimes also physical, resulting from the interaction between a living organism and a drug, characterised by behavioural and other responses that always include a compulsion to take the drug on a continuous or periodic basis in order to experience its psychic effects, and sometimes to avoid the discomfort of its absence. Tolerance may or may not be present. A person may be dependent on more than one drug.

Physical dependence is a state which occurs only with certain classes of drug, notably the opiates, barbiturates and minor tranquillizers. It requires a period of regular use before dependence is produced. Over time, the body becomes accustomed to the presence of the drug and adjusts so as to continue working as normally as possible. If the drug is then suddenly removed, the body is thrown off balance and takes some time to re-establish equilibrium, a process which manifests itself in more or less unpleasant withdrawal symptoms. The severity and characteristics of the withdrawal syndrome vary from drug to drug and can be greatly affected by psychological and situational factors. The myth of 'one shot and you're a junkie' is precisely that, as is the common belief (assiduously propagated by some drug takers) that the existence of physical dependence and the horrors of withdrawal make it impossible for heroin users to give up their habit. *Tolerance* refers to the way in which the body adjusts its functioning as it becomes accustomed to the drug's presence, so that larger doses are required to produce the same effect. Tolerance can develop to both desired and undesired effects, although not necessarily at the same rate or to the same extent. The usefulness of the concept of physical dependence (see Figure 3.1) as an explanation of the continued destructive use of drugs is a matter of some dispute (Peele 1985).

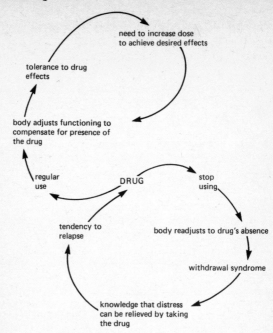

Figure 3.1 Physical dependence

Considerably more important in sustaining drug use is *psychological* dependence (see Figure 3.2). People can become psychologically dependent on almost any substance, from food to heroin, and sometimes no substance need be involved at all, as in the case of compulsive gambling or destructive relationships (Peele and Brodsky 1975). People can be said to exhibit psychological dependence on a drug when they have a strong desire or craving to continue taking it and find it difficult or seemingly impossible to desist, despite the negative effects stemming from the use. Their difficulties are not caused simply by the chemical properties of the drug: no substance really has the power to take away a person's will and power of choice. Rather it is a question of the role that the *drug experience* has come to play in their lives, so that the only way which they can see of coping with themselves or the world is to continue to take the drug. However painful their lives, however destructive they acknowledge their drug use to be, they still believe that without it their lives would be even more unsupportable. It is this belief, rather than the problems of physical dependence, which sustains their pattern of behaviour and makes it so difficult for them to give up drugs, as is shown by the enormous difficulties which users can encounter with drugs like the amphetamines that strictly speaking do not produce physical dependence at all.

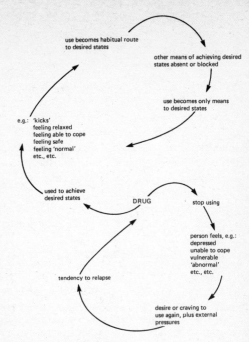

Figure 3.2 Psychological dependence

For dependent users, their drug use is the central organizing feature of their lives, their only, or only reliable, means of attaining desired psychological states, of feeling relatively normal, of coping with their internal and external environments. Deprived of the drug experience, they will feel abnormal, depressed, vulnerable and unable to cope. Such feelings provide strong motivation to resume drug use.

The line between dependent and non-dependent drug use is not a sharp one and many users will oscillate between these states over time, as their social and psychological circumstances alter.

The problem drug taker
Difficulties can and do arise long before the stage of dependence is reached. Intoxication and excessive consumption contribute to these, and Chapters 1 and 2 drew attention to the role of legal and social factors. The Advisory Council on the Misuse of Drugs (ACMD1982) clearly had these considerations in mind in its call for a fully multi-disciplinary approach to the problems of drug misuse and in its definition of the 'problem drug taker' as

any person who experiences social, psychological, physical or legal problems related to intoxication and/or regular excessive consumption and/or dependence as a consequence of his own use of drugs or other chemical substances (excluding alcohol and tobacco).

The exclusion of alcohol and tobacco from the definition is a result of the Council's terms of reference; they could profitably be included. Indeed, the Council acknowledged its debt to the model of the problem drinker put forward by the Advisory Committee on Alcoholism (1978).

The model of the 'problem drug taker', although imperfect, has distinct advantages in practice over earlier formulations. It discourages an exclusive emphasis upon the problems of that minority of drug users who are truly dependent. It moves the emphasis from a substance-centred to a problem-centred approach, gives pointers to where problems may arise and to their possible causation, and safeguards us to some extent from the moral overtones of concepts such as 'addict' and 'drug abuser'. It emphasizes that the care of the problem drug taker is not exclusively or primarily a medical responsibility, providing

a working model which is understandable to those responsible for the provision of services. It emphasizes that problems from taking drugs arise from three related areas: dependence, regular excessive consumption and intoxication. Each of these elements of drug taking behaviour may present separately, but often in drug takers the three elements overlap. Each element produces its own specific social, medical and legal problems and separating these out can aid planning of individual treatments and relevant services. (ACMD 1982)

Despite these advantages, social workers should be aware that they will encounter clients whose problems arise not from intoxication, excessive use, or dependence, but simply from negative legal and social reaction to the discovery that they have used drugs at all.

General hazards which may arise from drug use

Many problems that drug users experience are not substance-specific, but arise from the method and circumstances of use. These circumstances include the prevailing social attitudes to drugs and the legal framework in which they are embodied.

AIDS and other problems stemming from the mode of administration

Injecting drug users, along with homosexuals and haemophiliacs, are a high-risk group for contracting Acquired Immune Deficiency Syndrome (AIDS). The HIV virus responsible for the disease is spread through intimate contact with body fluids, principally by exchange of blood or semen. The prevalence rate for the presence of HIV antibody in those drug users who have been tested varies widely in different areas: from 51% in

Edinburgh (Robertson *et al.* 1986) to 0.6% in south London (Webb *et al.* 1986). Of the 686 cases of AIDS diagnosed to January 1987, 16 involved injecting drug use.

Users are at risk of HIV infection if they share injecting equipment with others who are already carriers, unless stringent precautions are taken to sterilize equipment between each injection. The risk increases with the frequency of sharing, with the numbers of people with whom sharing is practised and with the proportion of them who are HIV carriers. Those who have shared in the past, but no longer do so, may still have become infected. Concern about the spread of AIDS among drug users and the possibility of them acting as a bridge for transmitting the HIV virus into the general population has prompted calls for sterile needles and syringes to be made more available in an attempt to minimize the incidence of sharing. In early 1987 the government announced that it was setting up a number of pilot schemes along these lines.

Although most attention has focussed on the role of needle-sharing, sexual activity can also spread the virus. It is not uncommon for drug users, both male and female, to support their habit through prostitution, so providing another route for the introduction of the HIV virus into the drug-taking community. Injecting and non-injecting users and their sexual partners and contacts, whether or not they use drugs, are at risk if someone in the chain is an HIV carrier. Consequently, workers have a responsibility to provide their clients with information on how to reduce the risk by modifying both injecting and sexual practices.

Another danger can arise when needle-sharing is added to unsterile injection practice. A high percentage of injecting drug users are carriers of hepatitis (either hepatitis B, or non-A, non-B hepatitis), a potentially serious and highly infectious disease. Heptatitits is spread through body fluids, so that sexual partners, those sharing needles with an infected person, and workers may be at risk. Services which see a significant number of injecting drug users would be well advised to institute health and safety procedures to minimize the risk to staff and other clients. An effective hepatitis policy will be sufficient to prevent infection by the far less easily transmitted HIV virus.

Injecting is by far the most physically hazardous route of administration, but no mode of usage is risk-free. Snorting cocaine can lead to irritation and eventual destruction of the nasal septum, which although not fatal, is at least painful and unaesthetic. With many drugs, however they are used, there is a danger of an overdose which may prove fatal. Impaired judgement or awareness while under the influence of a drug increases the likelihood of accidents. Those for whom drug use is the central feature of their lives are likely to pay little attention to their general health, and so present suffering from undernourishment and vitamin deficiencies – conditions particularly likely to manifest themselves in the case of 'speed freaks', since the amphetamines act as appetite suppressants. Drug effects may also mask the signs of other illnesses, not necessarily directly related to drug use. The depressant action upon the respiratory system of the opioids and barbiturates makes their users particularly susceptible to illnesses such as pneumonia. Workers should be aware of the possibility of physical illness or debility and discuss with clients the issue of getting a medical check-up.

Contrary to popular opinion, a person injecting even quite large quantities of pharmaceutically pure heroin under sterile conditions could be expected to live to a ripe old age without experiencing any serious problems, apart from chronic constipation. However, few users are in this position. Usually, they will be taking either impure drugs, such as street heroin, or drugs which are not intended to be injected, such as Tuinal or Diconal, and administering them in ways which pay scant attention to the niceties of hygiene. Such practices lay users open to a variety of hazards.

Most 'street' drugs are adulterated to some degree. Heroin is usually 'cut' or diluted with glucose, but sometimes less innocuous substances are introduced. These 'cutting agents' and fillers in pharmaceutical drugs can cause thrombophlebitis when injected into a vein, as can barbiturates. Heavy injectors, having run out of veins in their arms, will move on to injecting in their legs and feet and, in extreme cases are forced to use hazardous sites such as the jugular or femoral veins, which are found close to the corresponding arteries. A mistaken injection into an artery will have serious and potentially fatal effects. Missing a vein can lead to irritation of the surrounding tissues and the formation of a sterile abscess. Barbiturate users are particularly prone to develop unsightly and unpleasant ulcers – the so-called 'barb burn'. In addition, unsterile injection techniques may result in an infected abscess. Intravenous or intra-arterial injection can give rise to gangrene and subsequent amputation of all or part of a limb. Unsterile techniques (using tap water, or water from a toilet bowl to dissolve the drug, for example) may lead to septicaemia and endocarditis.

Social and legal hazards
Either because of their direct effects, or because of social reactions, the use of drugs can lead users to suffer from a variety of problems. Drug use may adversely affect their work, leading to poor time-keeping or absenteeism. Because of this or because of the social stigma attached to drug use, they may lose their job. Unemployment or the cost of their habit may result in debt, with services being cut off and goods repossessed. Rent or mortgage arrears may eventuate in the loss of accommodation and homelessness, which in turn will create a further downward spiral of problems. Behavioural changes associated with drug use may cause strains in relationships between parents and children. Marriages and other partnerships may find themselves under

intolerable strain. Parenting may suffer and drug users find themselves faced with the possibility or actuality of their children being taken into care. Heavy involvement in drug use may lead to increasing social isolation, most of the user's contacts being with other drug takers. The unauthorized possession of controlled drugs is itself an offence and, in addition, many regular users become involved in illegal activities to support their habit, including drug dealing, shoplifting, burglary and prostitution and are prosecuted as a result, thus adding the burden of a criminal record to their other troubles. The ability to cope constructively with any or all of these problems may be diminished due to the effects of drugs and the spiral of deterioration be reinforced.

These problems – financial, legal, housing, family, marital, or social – will be familiar to social workers, since they do not differ in kind from the problems presented by the generality of non-drugusing clients. Lest the picture painted above appear too gloomy, it should be said that most drug takers do not experience all of these problems, or do so only to a minor extent. Where problems do occur, their severity will be influenced not only by the pattern and intensity of drug-taking, but also by the personal, social and financial resources of the drug taker. In general, the poor and under-privileged suffer earlier and more severely.

4 Drugs and Their Effects

Heroin and the other opiates

The opium poppy (*papaver somniverum*) is the ultimate source of a group of drugs called the opiates, of which heroin is currently the most prominent example. Others are morphine, codeine and opium itself, the sticky exudate of the poppy head. Purely synthetic drugs with similar effects (often referred to as opioids) include methadone (Physeptone), dipipanone (Diconal), pethidine, dextromoramide (Palfium) and dihydrocodeine (DF118). Although differing in strength and duration of action, there is a strong family resemblance between all of these substances. They are all, to a greater or lesser extent, powerful analgesics (hence heroin is used in the management of terminal cancer patients; morphine is included in the medical kits of mountain rescue teams; and Diconal has an established place in the treatment of chronic back pain). Their ability to suppress the cough reflex makes codeine a common ingredient of cough medicines. They affect the gastro-intestinal system; kaolin and morphine mixture is a time-honoured remedy for diarrhoea. Last but not least, methadone and other opioids are used as substitute drugs in the treatment of heroin dependency.

The vast majority of opiate dependants coming to medical notice are dependent upon heroin. Other opiates are, however, widely available on the street. There is a flourishing market in medically prescribed methadone; Diconal, although less prominent than in former years, is still to be found for sale; dihydrocodeine (DF118, a less powerful opioid) is popular and is often used by addicts whose drug of choice is heroin, to tide them over periods when the latter is not available.

Particularly when it is injected into a vein, many non-medical users of heroin experience an initial short-lived, very intense feeling, known as the 'rush', sometimes likened to an orgasm, followed by a longer-lasting euphoria, a calm and relaxed distancing from pain, both mental or physical. This cocoon-like well-being, where problems although still present do not have the power to disturb, makes the heroin experience extraordinarily attractive to many users.

Pure heroin is a white powder. Street heroin is invariably 'cut' or diluted with some other substance, usually glucose powder. Ranging in colour from beige to brown, its purity can vary widely between samples, but averages about 40%, in England, as compared to 5-10% in the United States.

Heroin can be taken in many ways: sniffed, smoked, swallowed, or injected. The most common method of use at the moment is to place the powder on silver foil, heat it with a match, and inhale the fumes through a tube. This is known as 'chasing', or 'chasing the dragon', a poetic description of Chinese origin. Although widespread, this is not a very cost-effective method of use and there is a tendency to graduate to injecting, with all its associated dangers.

Tolerance to heroin builds up quite quickly if the drug is regularly used and dependence can develop whatever the means of administration, although it takes some weeks of regular use for this to happen. Some people use heroin only occasionally and do not become dependent. Others, although no one knows how many, use regularly without having to increase the dose. Heroin overdoses can lead to death if the drug is purer than expected, or if the user has lost tolerance due, say, to a spell in prison. Mixing heroin and alcohol is particularly dangerous and may be the main cause of most so-called 'heroin overdose' deaths (Gossop 1982).

Few conditions are so surrounded with mythology as the heroin withdrawal syndrome. Both users and the media seem determined to exaggerate its horrors. In fact, withdrawal may best be likened in most cases to a bad dose of flu, something which is undoubtedly unpleasant enough, but which falls well short of the extremes of agony and degradation so often and so lovingly described. Symptoms may include runny nose and eyes, yawning, sweating, hot flushes, tremor, gooseflesh (hence the expression 'cold turkey'), restlessness, nausea and vomiting, diarrhoea, increased body temperature and blood pressure, increased respiratory rate, dehydration, muscle spasms and cramps. The chance of it leading to death is extremely remote. Withdrawal symptoms will appear within a few hours of the last dose, peak after about twelve hours and be over within a few days, although a number of less intense symptoms, such as disturbed sleep and perhaps depression may continue for some months. The severity of the withdrawal depends upon the size of the habit, but is also greatly influenced by users' expectations and fears about what they will have to go through and by the circumstances in which it occurs. For many users, the fear of withdrawal is the primary factor motivating continued use. Although usually not strictly necessary in physical terms (a major exception being pregnancy), gradual withdrawal under medical supervision is indicated where clients are too vulnerable, either psychologically or because of their situation, to have a reasonable chance of succeeding on their own.

Given its fearsome reputation, it is perhaps hard to accept that in itself heroin is a relatively benign drug. In terms of potential for physical harm, alcohol far outstrips it. 'The dangers of heroin addiction owe far more to the psychology of the addict and the ways in which addicts use the drug, than to any property inherent in the drug itself' (Gossop 1982). To which factors might be added the way in which society views both the drug and the addict.

Barbiturates and other sedatives

The barbiturates comprise a large family of drugs derived from barbituric acid. They are used medically as sedatives and hypnotics, as short-acting anaesthetics, and as a treatment for epilepsy. As awareness of their dangers has grown, their employment as anxiolytics and 'sleeping tablets' has declined in favour of the use of the minor tranquillizers. They are central nervous system depressants, which in small doses induce relaxation and reduce anxiety, and in larger amounts induce sleep.

Barbiturates have never acquired the aura of spurious glamour that surrounds heroin, perhaps because of their very familiarity – in 1968 over 17 million prescriptions for them were issued in England and Wales – and they were only controlled under the Misuse of Drugs Act in 1985, despite the fact that they had long been known as drugs of abuse.

The most commonly abused barbiturates are preparations such as Tuinal, Nembutal and Seconal. When taken 'non-medically', they produce a state closely akin to drunkenness: loss of coordination, slurred speech, confusion and sometimes aggressive or self-pitying behaviour and a lapse into unconsciousness. Other drugs, chemically unrelated but similar in effect to the barbiturates, include Mandrax, Doriden and Heminevrin.

Heavy barbiturate dependence is the most dangerous form of drug use. Tolerance to the lethal effects of the drug does not increase to anything like the extent that it increases to the effects which users are looking for, so the risk of fatal overdose is high and made more likely by the confused state brought on by heavy use. The dangers are increased if barbiturates are taken together with an opiate, or with alcohol, a particulary common combination. As with alcohol, users are prone to periods of amnesia, referred to as 'blackouts'. Physical dependence readily develops and the withdrawal syndrome is much more serious than with the opiates. It begins within a day of cessation of use (or even a decrease in the habitual dose) and symptoms include anxiety, twitching, trembling of the hands, dizziness, distortions of vision, nausea, postural hypotension (a drop in blood pressure on standing), seizures closely resembling epileptic seizures ('fitting'), delirium, and potentially coma and death. Barbiturate dependants, unlike heroin users, should never be encouraged to withdraw on their own: if at all possible, withdrawal should take place under medical supervision.

Barbiturates are either swallowed or injected. The latter practice is thankfully less common than it once was, since it is likely to result in ulceration and abscess formation. It is also not uncommon for faulty injection practices to require subsequent amputation of a limb. Due to their confused and comatose state, barbiturate users are also prone to accidents, such as falling asleep next to an electric fire and suffering traumatic burns.

Almost anyone who has had anything to do with 'barb freaks' will confess that, because of the extreme physical and behavioural effects of their drug use and the degree of psychological and social havoc which they exhibit, they can be extraordinarily difficult and depressing clients to work with, requiring a great deal of painstaking work often with little to show for it except the satisfaction of keeping them alive. However, the work of the City Roads Crisis Intervention Unit and other agencies has shown that much can be achieved, given patience and skill. (Jamieson, Glanz and MacGregor 1984).

Minor Tranquillizers

The minor tranquillizers, or benzodiazepines, are a group of drugs, including Valium, Librium, Ativan and Mogadon among many others, whose main medical uses are as anxiolytics and sedatives. They have largely replaced the barbiturates for these purposes, due to their greater margin of safety in overdose.

Benzodiazepines account for about 10% of all NHS prescriptions and in recent years there has been much disquiet about their wholesale prescribing by doctors. In 1983, some 23 million benzodiazepine prescriptions were issued by general practitioners in England. One in seven adults take them at some time during the year and one in forty take them throughout the year. Twice as many women as men are prescribed them (ISDD 1985). In its Annual Report for 1982-3, the Medical Research Council commented:

> they are often prescribed in situations in which the medical problem, if it exists at all, is only a minor component of the patient's total predicament.
>
> As symptoms during the withdrawal period are common enough to be the rule, patients themselves are motivated to continue to seek such prescription. However, 50 per cent of repeat prescriptions are given without consultation. (MRC 1983)

Both physical and psychological dependence can develop, even at therapeutic doses. Tolerance develops to their effects, and after a few weeks they may become ineffective in relieving anxiety or inducing sleep. Paradoxical effects of increased anxiety and irritability are sometimes found, due to a disinhibiting effect like that associated with alcohol. Impaired coordination and drowsinesss are commonly reported side-effects, and confusion, headaches, double vision, dizziness and nausea also sometimes occur. A proportion of users find it extremely difficult to stop and may experience distressing and protracted withdrawal symptoms, including anxiety, sleeplessness, perceptual distortions, depression, dysphoria, nausea and vomiting and, if the dose has been high, convulsions and fits. Medical thought now believes that, as a general rule, minor tranquillizers should only be prescribed for short periods, as their efficacy as sleeping pills can decline after about two weeks and their ability to control anxiety become ineffective after four months (ISDD 1984).

It has been estimated (SCODA 1986) that as many as 250,000 people have serious problems associated with their use of minor tranquillizers. It follows that benzodiazepines are likely to feature in the majority of drug-related cases seen by social workers in non-specialist positions. In many such cases, clients are unlikely spontaneously to volunteer that their drug use is a factor in the situation, and careful assessment procedures will be necessary if the possible contribution of the drug is not to be overlooked.

Because tranquillizer-users usually obtain their drugs on prescription and their use is seen as medically justified, neither the legal complications associated with the use of many other drugs, nor those difficulties which stem from the social disapproval and stereotyping of 'illegal' drug use will be present. Nevertheless, such clients may still experience great problems, either because of unwanted side effects and the difficulties they encounter when they try to stop using, or because continued use hampers their efforts to deal with problems or adds to them. As a short-term palliative for stress or insomnia, the benzodiazepines can be useful, but their use for extended periods is increasingly frowned upon.

Valium and similar drugs are also commonly used by heroin users as a form of self-medication during withdrawal and to 'fill the gap' when their preferred drug is not available.

Amphetamines and cocaine

Amphetamines are stimulants. Their use gives enhanced feelings of alertness, confidence and intelligence, increases physical endurance and postpones fatigue. Until these drugs were more strictly controlled in the 1960s, long-distance lorry drivers, students revising for exams, and harassed housewives, amongst many others, found these properties useful. Millions of tablets were distributed to troops in the Second World War. Excellent suppressors of appetite, they have been widely used and misused as 'slimming pills', although their use for this purpose is now not recommended. Indeed, there are now few if any medical indications for their use, except in the treatment of the rare complaint of narcolepsy.

These properties, attractive as they are, explain both the popularity of the amphetamines as recreational drugs and the aptness of the slang name 'speed'. Unfortunately, there are also distinct disadvantages to amphetamine use. Whether or not amphetamines produce physical dependence is a matter of debate, and of little importance, since there is no dispute that they are prone to give rise to strong psychological dependence. Regular heavy users usually, although not invariably, appear restless and agitated. They may talk a great deal, rapidly and to little effect. Constant use can produce irritability, anxiety and irrational feelings of persecution, sometimes culminating in a psychotic state similar to acute paranoid schizophrenia. This condition usually disappears quickly when use ceases. Regular users are often underweight and haggard, since they are burning energy faster than normally, not eating enough and going without sleep for long periods. In consequence, it is not surprising that when they stop taking the drug, they will experience exhaustion, hunger, prolonged but disturbed sleep and, sometimes, deep depression. The experience may be so unpleasant that there is a strong compulsion to start using again.

Amphetamines are often used on an occasional basis: at weekends, say, to enhance social interaction at a party, or to increase stamina for a hard night at the disco. In such cases, the more extreme negative effects described above would not be expected to occur. They are consequent upon heavier long-term use, which is much more widespread than is commonly believed. It is curious that very little attention has been paid to the amphetamines, since they are almost certainly used by more people than any other 'illegal' drug, with the exception of cannabis. Most forms of the drug available at present are illegally manufactured, either in pill form, or as a white powder know as 'sulphate', although pharmaceutical preparations such as Durophet and Dexedrine are still to be found. Other drugs with similar properties include Ritalin, a drug whose effects are to all intents and purposes identical to the amphetamines, and Tenuate Dospan, a somewhat milder stimulant. Amphetamines can be sniffed, swallowed, or injected. Since most users are unlikely to come to the attention of a doctor, the popularity of injecting amongst them is a worrying factor when considering the spread of AIDS.

If the amphetamines have remained sunk in public apathy, the same cannot be said for their more glamorous sister cocaine, which bids fair to take over heroin's mantle as public enemy number one. Cocaine, which until recently was a drug confined to the rich and trendy ('Cocaine is God's way of telling you that you are earning too much', as the saying goes), has moved simultaneously on to the streets and into the sermons of Fleet Street leader writers. Cocaine is an alkaloid, derived from the coca shrub (*Erythroxylum coca*), the leaves of which have traditionally been chewed by the inhabitants of the Andean region to promote stamina and suppress hunger. In Western countries, cocaine is usually taken as its hydrochloride and can be either snorted or injected. A relatively simple chemical process, known as 'freebasing' produces the free alkaloid, which is then smoked. This form of the drug is believed to give a more intense 'hit', with a correspondingly increased risk of strong psychological dependence. Recently, more sophisticated techniques have produced 'crack', an easily marketed form of cocaine freebase, which seems to have gained an all but unbreakable hold on the minds of journalists and politicians.

Cocaine use has undoubtedly become more common in the United Kingdom during the 1980s and its use has spread to all social classes. Most use is probably on an occasional or recreational basis. Hysteria aside, experience in the United States indicates that the cocaine habit can be painfully hard to break, at least when cocaine is smoked or injected rather than snorted. The drug's effects are similar to, but more intense and short-lived than the amphetamines'. The resulting temptation to repeat the dose at frequent short intervals, combined with its high price, mean that cocaine use is likely to be more socially and economically disruptive to the user's life. Unlike the amphetamines, tolerance does not develop to any extent. The unwanted side-effects are also close to those of the amphetamines and will not be further detailed here. Cases of death due to overdosing do occur, but are rare.

Hallucinogens
Although there are many substances which have a hallucinogenic effect, the only ones regularly available in the United Kingdom are LSD (lysergic acid diethylamide, or 'acid') and the so-called 'magic mushrooms'.

The primary effect of LSD is not upon mood, but perception. Sounds and colours are intensified, sometimes with the added phenomenon of kinaesthesia, where colours are perceived as sounds, smells as colours. Perceptions of time and space may undergo radical alteration. More or less fantastic illusions, pleasant or unpleasant, may be experienced. Users may seem to find themselves face to face with God, in tune with the universe, or, conversely, totally isolated in an alien and terrifying environment. But it should not be assumed that they always meet with, or even seek, such trancendental situations: this would be to over-solemnize what for many is often just an enjoyable experience. To a large extent, the tone of the hallucinogenic experience or 'trip' is set by the pre-existing mood and circumstances of the user. In congenial surroundings and feeling good about themselves, users are unlikely to experience a 'bad trip', although this is not an invariable rule. On the other hand, taking LSD to try to overcome one's unhappiness, or in threatening circumstances, is likely to lead to an unpleasantly negative result. 'Bad trips' are best dealt with by calm reassurance and support and do not normally require medical attention.

LSD has been sold in a bewildering variety of forms: as microdots, as tablets or capsules (most of which consist of inert filler, since the effective dose of the drug is almost vanishingly small), or as pieces of paper or transfers impregnated with the drug. The effect of a trip lasts several hours. Given what a powerful drug it is (an ordinary dose might be between 50-200 micrograms), it is perhaps surprising what a small percentage of its users come to harm. Stories of people throwing themselves from tower-blocks under the delusion that they can fly may have some basis in fact, but such behaviour is very much the exception. More obvious hazards exist for people operating machinery or driving a car while under the influence. Occasionally, probably with individuals who are already borderline psychotics, a bad trip results in a serious mental illness. A more common after-effect is the 'flashback', a vivid replay of LSD-induced experiences some time after the 'trip' has finished. This can be extremely worrying, but is seldom dangerous: sufferers can be reassured that flashbacks decrease in frequency with time and usually stop recurring altogether within a year.

LSD is not a drug of dependence and its physical effects are minimal. No convincing evidence of long-term physical harm, such as brain or chromosomal damage, exists, despite a somewhat over-enthusiastic hunt for it by many researchers.

In Britain, several species of fungi occur which contain hallucinogenic substances. The Liberty Cap mushroom (*Psylocybe semilanceata*) is perhaps the most commonly used and contains the substance psylocybin, a fairly potent hallucinogen. The effect of eating these mushrooms is like a rather milder LSD trip. In low doses they produce a degree of hilarity and giggling (as well as stomach-ache and nausea); higher levels produce more authentically hallucinogenic states. The main danger users face is probably picking the wrong mushroom by mistake. It says something about the lure of altered consciousness that the traditional British phobia to fungi not bought in a shop is routinely set aside by many of our young people.

Due to a quirk of the law, it is not illegal to pick, possess, or eat 'magic mushrooms', but is an offence to dry them, boil them, or otherwise alter their natural state, since such activities amount to 'making a preparation of a controlled substance' under the Misuse of Drugs Act.

Cannabis

Cannabis, also known as marijuana, hashish, hash, dope, blow, ganja and a host of other names, is by far the most commonly used of all recreational drugs. Offences concerning cannabis accounted for 79% of those found guilty or cautioned for breaches of the Misuse of Drugs Act in 1985. Cannabis is obtained from the leaves and tops of the Indian Hemp plant (*Cannabis Sativa*).

In this country, it is most commonly sold in the form of cannabis resin (hashish or hash), a brownish or black slightly tarry substance. It is also to be found as herbal cannabis (marijuana or 'grass') and sometimes as 'cannabis oil', a concentrated liquid prepared from the resin. It is usually smoked, either on its own or mixed with tobacco, but can be eaten, or drunk as a tea. The main psychoactive ingredient is tetrahydrocannabinol.

The effects of cannabis, various and greatly influenced by the user's underlying mood and expectations and by situational factors, are usually experienced as mild and pleasant: a sense of relaxation, well-being, talkativeness and laughter, sometimes accompanied by mild distortions of perception. With stronger doses more pronounced perceptual distortions occur. Many users report that use enhances their appreciation of music. Negative effects commonly reported include panic attacks and paranoia. Cannabis affects short-term memory and can distort judgement of time and distance, so its consumption while undertaking tasks which require concentration, or while driving or operating machinery, has obvious disadvantages.

It is fair to say that most users enjoy their use and do not see it as a problem, except insofar as cannabis is a controlled drug and its users therefore liable to prosecution under the Misuse of Drugs Act. Despite much research, there is little firm evidence that cannabis has long-term ill-effects, either physical or mental. In particular, the existence of a specific 'cannabis psychosis' remains unproven (Gossop 1982), although such diagnoses are not uncommon. Fatal overdose is unknown.

For the last two decades, cannabis has been the subject of intense political debate, its supporters presenting it as a drug with practically no drawbacks and demanding its legalization, its detractors seeking out each shred of evidence which might be used to damn it. Such polarization is unhelpful. In the past, cannabis has had a number of medical uses, but today strongly held attitudes prevent its employment, despite convincing evidence showing its usefulness in the treatment of glaucoma and in alleviating the side effects of chemotherapy. Most of the problems which users experience are due, not to the direct effects of cannabis, but to the drug's legal status and the prevailing attitudes surrounding its use. On the other hand, although most people come to no great harm from their cannabis use, no substance is without its dangers. A small percentage of users find it impossible to cope without the drug and use it at frequent intervals to get through their day. Such cases are not common, but should not be brushed aside when they occur, as sometimes happens when the worker has an uncritically enthusiastic view of the harmlessness of cannabis.

Solvents

Solvent abuse or 'glue sniffing' as it is commonly called, can involve the inhalation of a wide variety of volatile organic substances, including glues, thinners for typewriter correction fluids, dry cleaning agents, petrol, aerosols and butane gas lighter refills. The effects are broadly similar to alcohol intoxication, though less long-lasting: euphoria, loss of inhibitions, disorientation, impaired coordination, slurred speech and loss of control, and unconsciousness. In addition, some users seek pseudo-hallucinogenic states, often referred to as 'dreams' or 'illusions'.

In most cases, solvent sniffing is a short-lived activity of children and adolescents, often carried out in a group; a fashion which comes and goes. A minority of users will continue to use on a long-term basis, developing a true psychological dependence. Although the focus of concern has been upon the younger age groups, people in their twenties, thirties, or even forties may also use solvents, sometimes as a cheaper substitute for alcohol.

Methods of administration vary with the substance. Glues are usually inhaled from a small plastic or crisp bag placed over the nose and mouth. Sometimes a larger plastic bag is placed over the head in addition, to increase the concentration of vapour, a practice which heightens the risk of suffocation, as does the spraying of aerosols and gases directly into the mouth. The use of some aerosol propellants and cleaning fluids carries a risk of heart failure, particularly if combined with exertion or excitement.

Short-term dangers include: suffocation from plastic bags over the head, from sniffing in places with poor ventilation, or from the inhalation of vomit while unconscious; accidents while intoxicated; and death due to the direct toxicity of the substance itself. Between 1981 and 1985, solvent-related deaths in the United Kingdom rose from 46 to 116. Fifty-three per cent of these were due to the direct toxic effect of the substance involved, rather than to suffocation or accidents (Anderson *et al.* 1986). Earlier research suggests that glues are somewhat safer in this respect than other substances (Anderson *et al.* 1985).

Less serious short-term side effects of solvent use are 'hangovers', bronchial and gastric problems, fatigue, forgetfulness and lack of concentration, appetite loss, mood swings, and skin rashes from contact with adhesives. Sniffers will sometimes develop a tremor of the hands, which will usually disappear on cessation of use.

Evidence of serious long-term physical damage is slim, perhaps surprisingly in view of the known effects of chronic exposure to low concentrations of many volatile organic substances in industrial settings:

> lasting damage attributable to solvent misuse seems extremely rare. In Britain, the evidence is limited to a few isolated cases, and surveys of groups of sniffers have not revealed any persistent medical consequences. (ISDD 1984)

Other over-the-counter and prescribed drugs
Although there are no reliable estimates of the numbers involved, many people of all ages regularly consume common over-the-counter and prescription medicines for the sake of their euphoriant, sedative or stimulant effects. Codeine linctus, Collis Browne's Chlorodyne and cough mixtures such as Actifed, Benylin and Phensydyl, for example, all contain psychoactive substances. Social workers should be alert to the occurrence of these less publicized forms of drug use among their clients, which may at times be creating or contributing to problems.

5 Theories of Drug Use

A drug is any substance which, when injected into a rat, gives rise to a learned paper. (Traditional saying)

Attempts to explain drug use have approached the problem from a bewildering variety of directions. Some theories emphasize the inherent properties of the drug itself. Others stress the physiological peculiarities of the user, conceived as either genetically determined or drug induced. Psychological explanations, particularly of a psychoanalytic or behaviourist persuasion, abound, while sociologists have not been slow to turn the spotlight on social and cultural factors. The result has been a voluminous and sometimes murky literature, in which it is only too easy to lose one's way.

Jaffe (1977) suggests that any completely adequate theory of drug misuse should be able to explain a spectrum of behaviours ranging from initial use, through casual and intensive use, to dependence and relapse. It scarcely seems necessary to go to these lengths. A theory of drug use is really an answer to the perennial question: 'why do people take drugs?' Implicitly, this is really three questions: (1) why do they take drugs? (2) why do some experience difficulties, as a result? and (3) why do some become addicted or dependent?

The first two questions are relatively easy to answer. The reasons why people take socially disapproved drugs are quite mundane. They are no different to the reasons why most of us take socially approved ones, like coffee, tobacco, or alcohol: because we enjoy the effects, to relax, for stimulation, to help us cope with problems, to escape, out of habit, to ease social interaction, because of social pressures, to conform, to help pass the time, from boredom, from curiosity, or to promote an image. These reasons may be strong enough for many of us to continue use even if problems occur and the disadvantages of so doing have become apparent. The immense toll taken by nicotine and the enormous damage to self, family and society caused by over-indulgence in alcohol should be sufficient proof of this. So it should not be surprising that the users of socially disapproved drugs should continue to take them when the problems that result seem clear to the outside observer and often to the users themselves. Drug use is as near to a human universal as one is likely to get. As long as the advantages (real or imagined) outweigh the disadvantages in the minds of users, they will continue to use. The third part of the question requires more extended discussion. It is complicated by the need to explain the occurrence of dependence upon several classes of drug, which may have little in common apart from their ability to influence mood. Confusion is worse confounded when the undeniable influence of social and cultural factors in determining what counts as 'addiction' or 'dependence' in a given situation is taken into account.

The most obvious explanation of the phenomenon of dependence is that the properties of a drug like heroin, say, are such as to automatically compel those who take it to repeat the experience. This theory, which recalls the stories of magic potions in folktale and myth, appears to be ineradicably inscribed in popular thought, and remains strongly entrenched in academic and medical circles, despite the fact that it is contradicted by a mass of evidence. Many people take heroin, and other so-called dependence-producing drugs on a casual basis, without either increasing the dose, or the frequency of their use (Zinberg 1984). This pattern is a matter of common observation with alcohol, but suggestions that it occurs with more socially disapproved drugs meet with great resistance. Furthermore, there is evidence to suggest that many people find the effects of opiates and other 'drugs of abuse' actively unpleasant and will not continue their use, even given the opportunity. Patients who have been prescribed large doses of opiates in the course of hospital treatment generally display neither withdrawal symptoms nor a craving to resume use upon discharge. Even more surprisingly, Zinberg (Zinberg *et al* 1978) has described the case of a physician who for many years used morphine four times a day, for ten months a year, refraining from use at weekends and during his annual holiday, without increasing his dosage and without experiencing serious withdrawal symptoms. It is also difficult to account, if dependence is the deterministic process suggested by this approach, for the experience of American troops during the Vietnam war, when heroin use reached endemic proportions among enlisted men (Robins *et al*. 1975). Some 50% had used heroin and 20% were judged to be dependent upon it. The US authorities were understandably alarmed by the prospect of large numbers of GI addicts returning to the States after their tour of duty, but in fact, once away from the pressures of the war, only some 14% relapsed to dependence after their return, although half continued to use on a casual basis. Examples such as this — inexplicable if heroin possesses the property of automatically producing addiction — have led many theorists to believe that dependence develops as the result of complex interactions between a drug, the physical and psychological constitution of the user, the situation in which drug use takes place and the cultural expectations surrounding use.

If the cause of dependence cannot be ascribed purely to the effects of the drug, and if only some of those exposed to the drug go on to become dependent, then the obvious next step is to try and discover if there are physical differences between individuals which could account for this. Some theories (Dole and Nyswander 1968) have suggested that vulnerability to becoming dependent upon drugs may be increased by the presence of a pre-existing biological abnormality (which may be genetic in origin). Such an abnormality might lead to drug use in one of two ways: either by producing a psychological or behavioural condition such as dysphoria or hyperactivity which increases the likelihood of drug use as a form of self-medication; or by manifesting itself as an enhanced positive reaction to the effects of drugs. The suggestion has been made that low levels of the endogenous opioid-like endorphins may make the opiates (and, indeed, other drugs) particularly attractive to affected individuals.

Alternatively, it has been postulated, notably by Dole and Nyswander (1968), that exposure to opiates leads to lasting drug-induced metabolic changes which in turn make continued use necessary. Once again, a decreased level of endorphin synthesis has been suggested as a possible mechanism.

In effect, such approaches seek to preserve the belief in the magical ability of drugs to enslave the user, but restrict this ability to the cases of individuals who are physiologically abnormal in some as yet undiscovered way. Despite much research, the existence of such abnormalities as a factor in dependence has not been convincingly demonstrated. Indeed, given the wide range of substances upon which people can become dependent, and the tendency of many to use a number of pharmacologically dissimilar substances either simultaneously or sequentially, it seems inherently unlikely that any single abnormality could be held accountable, and frankly incredible that evolution could have left humanity so vulnerable to dependence upon so many unrelated chemicals.

Behaviourist theories
If neither pharmacological nor physiological factors suffice, where are we to look for explanation of dependence? An alternative and highly favoured line of approach has been that provided by learning theory. Because of the opportunities offered for sophisticated experimental design, learning theorists have been leading and influential figures in the debate. Both positive and negative reinforcement has been seen as crucial, and both operant and Pavlovian conditioning have been called into play. Lindesmith (1968) has emphasized the importance of the addict's recognition of the need to avoid painful withdrawal symptoms in establishing and continuing dependency. Bejerot (1972) concentrates on the positive psychopharmacological effects of the opiates as reinforcers of use. Wikler (1973) combines both sources of re-enforcement and adds the idea of conditioned withdrawal symptoms as a further goad prodding the ex-user to relapse into renewed use. Behaviourist approaches tend to minimize the importance of pre-existing psychopathology or physiological peculiarities in the genesis of dependence and to retain an unquestioned belief in the power of drugs as reinforcers of behaviour, being in that sense merely an elaboration of the pharmacological approach, and so vulnerable to similar arguments.

Psychodynamic theories

Perhaps, then, the secret is to be found in the psychology of the user. Since Freud (who saw masturbation as the 'primary addiction' from which all others were derived), theorists of a psychoanalytic persuasion have produced theories to account for the phenomenon of addiction, often seeing addicts as fixated at the oral level of development as a result of unsatisfactory mother-child relations. Personality traits stemming from this maturational failure may include manipulativeness, passivity, dependence on others, and fear of heterosexual relationships. Sometimes addicts are seen as using drugs as a way of masking anxiety or aggressive drives with which they would otherwise be unable to cope.

An early writer in the field, Rado (1933) believed all drug dependents to suffer from a pre-existing psychological state of 'tense depression'. Later researchers (Chein *et al.* 1964) saw not only depression, but also anxiety, bewilderment, despair, panic, self-rejection and longing as important states and linked these with family background and the influence of community.

The idea that a distinct 'addictive personality' exists is an enticing one, but researchers who believe that they have succeeded in characterizing it have not generally had their findings confirmed by other workers. Drug users remain stubbornly heterogenous. The further question remains of whether such personality and character disorders as are found are causative of or consequent upon drug use. But this should not, as it sometimes does, particularly among those of a sociological bent, lead to the belief that personal pathology has no part to play in the genesis of problematic drug use. It may well be that people labouring under the handicap of a very diffuse range of psychological pressures find relief in some form of drug use.

More important than the search for the probably illusory 'addictive personality' is the fact that psychodynamic theories make a radical break with those already discussed by placing the emphasis not upon the inherent powers of the drug, but upon the role that its use plays in altering intrapsychic states in ways that the addict finds desirable. Such theories thus leave room for the observation that only some drug users progress to the stage where their use is compulsive, and provide an explanation of how that compulsive use can be seen to fulfil an adaptive function for the user. Going beyond the consideration of strictly psychological theorizing, many researchers (e.g. Chien *et al.* 1964) have pointed to the importance of familial, social and cultural factors. Zinberg (1984), has been prominent in drawing attention to the necessity of taking the contribution of drug, individual psychic factors (set) and the social context (setting) into account.

Sociological theories

Chein's (1969) observation that the heroin user's addiction provided 'a vocation around which [he could] build a reasonably full life' provides a bridge to an important strand of sociological thinking, that of drug use as a career, offering rewards analogous to those of more conventional strategies and enabling the user to establish a personal identity, albeit a deviant one. The serious drug user's life can indeed be a busy one: finding money for drugs, scoring, fixing, stealing, disposing of stolen property, dealing, avoiding the police, perhaps escaping detection by family and friends. Where more socially approved ways may be blocked, by personal or social pressures, the role of 'drug addict' may have attractions in itself, quite apart from the effects of the drug. Valuable as such insights are, it is sometimes difficult to see why drug use, rather than some less potentially self-destructive form of deviancy, is chosen. But sociological approaches to the problem are less concerned with explaining the phenomenon of dependence than with illuminating the ways in which drug use can be seen to make sense as an activity for those who indulge in it, or exploring the ways in which the social response to drug use affects users.

Young (1971) and Becker (1963) have shown how social reaction moulds the life experiences or self-conceptions of drug users through the processes of deviancy amplification and labelling. Auld, Dorn and South (1984) have drawn attention to the role of drug dealing as an element of the informal economic system in economically deprived areas.

Many theorists have stressed the association between social deprivation and drug use, a correlation which has been more obvious in the United States than in this country, where opiate users have been fairly evenly distributed across all social classes. However, although drug use is by no means a working-class monopoly, there are signs that run-down inner-city areas now have more than their fair share of drug problems, as of all others.

MacAndrew and Edgerton (1969) have illuminated the importance of cultural factors in determining not only social attitudes to drugs, but also the actual effects drugs have on users. They describe the enormous variation between cultures in the extent to which alcohol eventuates in aggressive and anti-social behaviour. Such findings are inexplicable from the currently dominant perspective which stresses the invariant effects of substances upon their users.

Perhaps the most important contribution of sociology to the debate lies in the insistence that 'drugs' and 'drug misuse' are not self-evident features of the natural world, but are socially constructed categories. Hence the necessity of including the social dimension in any discussion on 'addiction', a term which has changed its meaning in a protean fashion over the years. In previous times, an 'addict' was someone suffering from a defect of will, or of moral fibre, and censured or tolerated accordingly. In this century, addiction has mostly been conceptualized as an illness, its management as belonging in the domain of the medical profession. The realization that addiction sits uncomfortably within the rubric of 'illness' has helped towards the recognition that non-medical professionals can play an important and legitimate role in assisting addicted users to cope with their problems in more constructive ways.

When considering any theory, it is important to be aware of just what it is purporting to explain and whether its tenets are likely to be useful for the purposes in hand. For example, the rapid changes in experimental and recreational use in the United Kingdom over the past few years are poorly explained by theories which emphasize the role of biological or psychological traits within the population, since it seems highly unlikely that these could have changed dramatically enough to account for the observed increase in such behaviour. We would do better to look for social factors – such as increased drug availability, changed attitudes towards drug use and society, and changes in the attainability of desired social goals – as an explanation. To search for psychopathology in a client solely on the grounds that he or she is using cannabis once or twice a week would be ill-advised. On the other hand, when considering the case of an individual heavily and destructively dependent on heroin, although social factors may be of great importance, they are unlikely to provide the worker with a total picture of the individual's situation, and consideration of personal psychology would probably be called for.

In an attempt to bring some order into the jumble of competing theoretical approaches, Alexander and Hadaway (1982) have suggested that theories can be classified as examples of one or the other of two mutually exclusive models, which they call the 'exposure' and the 'adaptive' orientations. Their argument is couched in terms of the opiates, but can profitably be widened out to include dependency on any drug. The exposure orientation would then hold that drug addiction is a condition that occurs because the drug's inherent properties engender a powerful tendency towards subsequent, compulsive use; the adaptive orientation would claim that addiction is the result of an attempt on the user's part to adapt to chronic distress of any sort through the habitual use of drugs as a coping strategy. Alexander and Hadaway believe that the theoretical approaches within the adaptive orientation fit the known facts best and posit three conditions under which opiate use will develop into an addictive positive feedback loop:

(a)   opiates are used to adapt to distress,
(b)   the user perceives no better means of adaptation,
(c)   opiate use ultimately leads to an increase in the original
         distress.

They continue:

> The necessary and sufficient causes of opiate addiction, from an adaptive orientation, are the three listed above. These ...are obviously the outcome of a wide range of more remote processes such as the tasks expected of a person, the

adaptive patterns that are available to the person, personality, health, drug availability, cultural sanctions on drug use, and so forth. In terms of the adaptive orientation, the task of controlling drug addiction is one of determining how these remote processes affect the three immediate causal factors and of intervening when required.

An important benefit of the adaptive orientation is that it alerts us to the fact that not everyone who uses a drug will experience problems as a result, still less become addicted. The adaptive orientation suggests, in line with ordinary intuition, that some users will have a stronger need to cope and/or be faced with more overwhelming problems than others and that for such people their drug use will provide both a short-term escape and a source of further difficulties. Should the need to cope and the constraints upon the user, real or imagined, be strong enough, addiction will result.

This chapter has concentrated upon the problems of addiction. But addicts constitute a minority of all drug users and it must be stressed that problems can also arise which have no necessary connection with the presence or absence of a dependent or addictive state. Despite the welcome tendency today to play down the importance of the specific substance, it should not be forgotten that, like alcohol, most socially disapproved drugs have extremely powerful effects on mind or body (after all, that is why people take them), which can lead to severe difficulties for users who may suffer from no discernible social or psychological handicap whatever. As Zinberg says:

> ...greater problems do not necessarily arise from repeated use than from initial or nondependent use. The neophyte or infrequent drinker of alcohol or user of barbiturates may have an automobile accident or engage in a brawl while under the influence of booze or drugs. If he cannot learn to use a substance adaptively, he is no less a problem because he is not dependent. In fact, most of the drugs considered drugs of abuse (with the exception of alcohol and the barbiturates) are used with far greater control by regular, experienced users than by neophytes. (Zinberg, Harding and Apsler 1978).

In addition, as we have seen in the previous chapters, the use of such drugs, however harmless and well-controlled that use might be, in itself lays the user open to stigmatization and possible legal sanctions.

6 Services For Drug Users

No one service will be able to respond to all the needs of all drug takers. The range of possible problems and the heterogeneity of the client group ensure this. And a given client may need different services at different times. So there will be instances when client and worker identify problems, or areas for change and development, that can best be met by other services. Possible referral on should always be carefully considered and discussed with clients to ensure that they are clear about the reasons for referral and certain of its usefulness. For this to be possible, workers need to be knowledgeable about the full range of services in their locality and to cultivate contacts with them. An inappropriate or ill-considered referral can set the client up to fail, reducing self-worth and inducing cynicism about seeking further help. The client's apparent failure may then be interpreted by the worker as indicating a lack of motivation to attempt change.

In thinking about referring on, the following points should be borne in mind:

1. Clarification of areas of need in terms both of problem areas and of improving the client's quality of life. What service is best placed to respond?
2. Referral should never be an automatic process. The fact that a particular service has worked well in previous cases is no guarantee that it will be useful to this client. A direct appeal for referral by the client should always be talked through to try and ensure that it is appropriate. A worker's exasperation with a client, although a frequent reason for referring on, is not a good one.
3. Onward referral does not necessarily preclude the continued involvement of the worker: services may be complementary in what they can offer. The social worker may usefully provide continuity and support to clients while they undergo treatment, or after they leave an in-patient detoxification or rehabilitation programme. The worker's role may change over time, become redundant, or continue for many years.
4. Drug takers, as members of society, have a right to the facilities of services not specifically geared to problem drug use: legal advice agencies; adult literacy classes; further education opportunities; employment schemes, childcare support, and so on. The worker may have to take on an educational or advocative role on behalf of the client, as

services may be resistant if they know that drug use is a factor in the case.

5. Both when making an onward referral and when accepting a referral from another service, the client's interests will be best served if all sides are clear what the purpose of the referral is and what can be expected of it. Collaboration between agencies will help improve the continuity of care.

6. Referral procedures require interchange of information about the client and so raise issues of confidentiality. As far as possible, workers should only pass on information which is both relevant and necessary to the referral, and ensure that the client is aware of and agreeable to this happening.

7. Where a referral has apparently failed, the responsibility should not automatically be placed upon the client. The referral may have been inappropriate, the client poorly prepared or given inadequate information. The client's circumstances may have changed during the course of a protracted referral process. Despite genuine efforts, the client may not have been able to carry through the commitment. Clients may undergo several detoxifications or spend several apparently unfruitful spells in a rehabilitation house and gain a little from each experience, even though this may not be recognized at the time. Worker and client should explore what happened, looking for any positive elements that may have been present, making connections around what went wrong and why, and examining the implications for future work.

The aim of intervention: drug-freeness or harm reduction?
A random sample of the general public, if asked what should be the aim of work with drug users, would almost certainly reply, without any hesitation, that it should be to help them to stop. Opinion within the field itself is far less unanimous.

Many workers hold that their primary aims should be to minimize the degree of drug-related harm which users experience and to help them maximize their control over consumption. The reasons for this should be clear by this point. We live in a drug-using society and most of us take drugs in one form or another, and/or are habituated to substances to regulate or modify our moods. It seems arbitrary and unfair to impose a stringent requirement of total abstinence upon a particular group whose drug use happens to be, largely for cultural and historical reasons, socially unacceptable (see Chapter 2). Most users of controlled drugs come to little or no harm and what difficulties they do experience stem more from the force of social and legal reaction than from the intrinsic properties of the drugs they choose to take. Why then should they be forced to stop, except to satisfy the prejudices of a majority which in its use of alcohol is scarcely a model of sobriety? Might it not be better to seek to modify those prejudices and develop models of 'acceptable' drug use analogous to social models of acceptable drinking? For that proportion of users who do suffer serious harm, it has been argued that it is counterproductive to provide only treatment options orientated towards more-or-less immediate abstinence, as such an approach may deter users from seeking help, and pushes them further into illegal activities, so increasing rather than diminishing the sum total of drug-related harm.

Others argue equally passionately that, at least for those who are dependent upon drugs and whose lives are demonstrably suffering as a result, the only solution is to persuade and support them towards abstinence as quickly as possible. Adherents of this position would also hold that by placing abstinence at the forefront of their approach they are simultaneously reducing the sum of drug-related harm. Such arguments are sometimes, though far from invariably, backed up by the claim that drug dependence is an illness. It is symptomatic of the complexity of the issues that this belief has also been used to buttress the practice of maintaining drug users upon opiates.

Defenders of both viewpoints can muster formidable arguments in their defence. The danger arises from the possibility of either position developing into an orthodoxy which limits the options open to those seeking help with their drug problems. The long-running debate on the merits or demerits of maintenance prescribing, which is still far from settled, exemplifies this. In some areas, users approaching a drug clinic for help will be offered no option but short-term detoxification. In others, they will almost automatically be offered a maintenance prescription. Such blanket policies, even though introduced for the best of reasons, detract from the principle that the service should respond to the needs of the individual, not fit the individual to the service. The very heterogeneity of drug users, their circumstances, and their problems demand the widest possible mix of service responses if their needs are to be met adequately.

Specialist provision for drug users

The extent of specialist provision is far from uniform across the country. Some areas are comparatively well served by a range of facilities, others offer only a single model of service delivery, in still others there may be no provision at all. It should therefore not be assumed that examples of all the specialist services described below will be found in any given locality.

Drug dependence units

Most areas of the country are now served by a specialist drug dependence unit, usually referred to as a 'DDU', or 'drug clinic'. The clinics were set up following the recommendations of the Brain Committee (see Chapter 1) and were intended to take over completely the medical treatment of opiate dependants. In this they have been only partially successful.

There is no uniform pattern of service provided by DDUs. Most are based within psychiatric hospitals. The clinic will be in the charge of a consultant psychiatrist, usually assisted by social work, nursing and administrative staff. The premises, staff time and equipment available vary widely from clinic to clinic and the service they offer varies both with the policy of the individual unit and with the resources at its disposal. Most will provide out-patient detoxification for opiate dependants. In addition, some will have access to in-patient facilities. Others will *only* accept patients for in-patient detoxification, while a few offer more or less open-ended maintenance regimes. Although primarily orientated towards opiate problems, many provide some service for those dependent upon other classes of drug, for example in withdrawing from barbiturates. As an integral part of treatment, clinics provide social work support on an individual and sometimes a group basis, and will often have contacts with other specialist services in the locality, such as rehabilitation houses and advice and counselling agencies.

Some DDUs will accept self-referrals and referrals from social workers and members of allied professions, while others insist upon referral through a doctor. The demand on some clinics means that it may take some time to secure an initial appointment. A detailed case and drug history will be taken and the patient required to provide urine samples for testing to ensure that opiates are indeed being taken. A treatment plan will then be drawn up and agreed. Usually this will consist of an out-patient prescription of oral methadone on a reducing basis, aiming for complete detoxification at the end of a certain time, which may be a matter of weeks or months according to the clinic's assessment of the patient's needs and capabilities. This process ideally will be accompanied by a range of therapeutic interventions, perhaps including casework, individual and group psychotherapy, family therapy and social skills training.

If it seems unlikely that a patient can cope successfully in the community, or if there are medical indications for this, in-patient detoxification may be offered, either in a specialist unit, or in the psychiatric short-stay ward of a general hospital. Drug users are sometimes unhappy to be placed in a psychiatric ward, resenting what they see as stigmatization, but specialist NHS beds for detoxification are in short supply: in 1985, the Standing Conference on Drug Abuse estimated that there were only a hundred or so in the United Kingdom (SCODA 1985).

Clonidine, a drug used in the treatment of heart complaints, is sometimes used in withdrawal from the opiates, as in many cases it appears effective in masking withdrawal symptoms, although side effects need careful management. Naltrexone, an opiate antagonist which blocks the effects of heroin and other opiates has also been experimented with.

Most clinic doctors moved away from the clinics' original policy of long-term opiate maintenance during the mid-1970s. But some still regard it as a valid response to the needs of many, or even all, of their patients, reasoning that attempts to dragoon users into abstinence are counterproductive, forcing them on to the illegal market to feed their habit and deterring them from approaching services that provide little that they see as relevant to their needs.

The perennial debate on the desirability of long-term maintenance has been given fresh impetus as a result of concern about the role of injecting drug users in the spread of the HIV virus. This has posed dilemmas for all drug workers as to where their main priorities in patient or client care should lie. Should the prevailing emphasis in medical circles upon requiring users to become drug-free be upheld, or should priority be given to stemming the spread of AIDS and protecting injecting drug users from the hazards to which their activities lay them open? Given that AIDS poses much greater risks than continuing drug use, many would plump for the latter alternative. An implication of this is that the long-term maintenance of drug users, an option which has practically disappeared in many areas, will need to be considered again as a valid treatment response. The introduction of needle and syringe distribution schemes, designed to cut down the incidence of users sharing equipment, also carries with it the need to reassess the current orthodoxy of prescribing only non-injectable drugs to patients. In making such decisions, the health needs of individual drug users, some of whom may already be infected by the HIV virus, need to be taken into account, as well as those of the community at large.

Accident and Emergency Departments
General hospital accident and emergency departments are an important service for drug users suffering from the effects of an overdose and in immediate physical danger, injured while in an intoxicated state, or suffering from the physical complications of injecting drugs, such as abscesses or septicaemia.

General practitioners
Research carried out in 1985 disclosed that about one in five general practitioners attended an opiate user during the four-week period covered by the survey (Glanz and Taylor 1986). The estimated number of patients was 6000-9000, a third of whom were new to the doctor. Over half had been treated for six months or more, and opiate drugs were prescribed in almost a third of the cases.

General practitioners are excellently placed to provide a service to problem drug users, and a report by an expert medical group of the Advisory Council on the Misuse of Drugs warmly encouraged them to become involved (DHSS 1984). Such involvement would not only take pressure off over-stretched specialist services, but would also fit in with current trends towards providing care in the community. Apart from responding to the problems of dependence, the general practitioner also has an important role in dealing with the general health needs of drug-using patients, which often go untreated and add to the difficulties of change.

Unfortunately, many doctors in general practice are wary of accepting responsibility for the treatment of drug takers. The same survey which showed the extent of GPs' involvement also revealed their unease in this area of work. On the whole, they regarded opiate users as especially difficult to manage, less acceptable patients than others needing care, and as beyond their competence to treat. Most were relatively unwilling to take them on as patients. Their most common response was to refer the patient to a drug dependence unit or to general psychiatric services. These findings point to the need for more education and support to be provided for GPs. Where general practitioners are interested and where they work together with local statutory and non-statutory services, the results are encouraging.

Advice and counselling services
Advice and counselling services, or 'street agencies' as they are often called to emphasize their accessibility to clients, provide a strategic link in the network of services for those with drug problems. Unlike the DDUs, they have never restricted their brief to working primarily with opiate users, but have been prepared to work with all those suffering from drug-related problems, irrespective of the particular substance involved. Their voluntary status has meant that they are attractive to many users who are unwilling to take their problems to statutory services, and that they have been able to respond quickly and flexibly to changes in the drug scene. They provide services to users, families and friends and to other agencies, both specialist and non-specialist, statutory and non-statutory. Their work includes giving advice and help with practical problems of accommodation, employment, social security and the law; counselling and casework, on a short- or long-term basis, thus functioning as a non-residential resource for rehabilitation within the community; referring on to appropriate services and receiving referrals in turn. Advice and consultancy to workers in non-drug specialist and generic agencies also figures largely, and some have pioneered an educational and training role. Street agencies see their objective as the amelioration of drug-related harm and the improvement of clients' quality of life. They do not, therefore, demand that clients exhibit a commitment to drug-freeness.

Since the increased availability of funding in the 1980s, the small number of long-established street agencies such as the Hungerford Drug Project, the Blenheim Project, the Community Drug Project and the Lifeline Project have been able to expand their activities and have been joined by new services operating along similar lines.

The 1980s have also seen the rise of telephone advice and counselling services, some of which also undertake face-to-face work. Some, such as the various Turning Point Drugline agencies, employ one or two full-time staff, plus volunteers. Others depend solely on the services of volunteers.

The Advisory Council on the Misuse of Drugs (ACMD 1982) recommended the establishment of district drug problem teams and this recommendation has been followed through in many areas by the creation of community drug teams. The composition and objectives of such teams varies, but they typically consist of a social worker and a community psychiatric nurse, with some medical back-up, and provide both direct services and a point of entry into local generic and specialist services where appropriate. Some teams are based in hospital premises, others in the community.

Self-help groups
Also notable has been the emergence of community and self-help groups. Some of these exist to provide help and support for the families and friends of drug takers, or for those experiencing difficulties with their use of minor tranquillizers. Others function as pressure groups. Yet others provide direct services for drug users.

Since its introduction to the UK in 1980, Narcotics Anonymous has become a rapidly growing source of help for problem drug users. Families Anonymous provides a similar support to the relatives and friends of drug takers. As the names imply, NA and FA groups are run on the same lines as Alcoholics Anonymous and Al-Anon. NA members include those who have experienced problems with the whole range of psychoactive drugs, including alcohol and the only requirement for membership is the desire to stop using (Wells 1987). Addiction is characterized as an illness to be overcome by following the twelve steps of the programme. This involves members recognizing that they are ill, that total abstinence is the only means of halting and reversing the effects of their condition and that placing reliance upon a 'higher power' (conceived in terms of the group itself, the Christian God, or some other spiritual power) is essential to this process. Those who have succeeded in achieving drug-freeness are referred to not as being 'cured', but as 'recovering addicts'.

Residential rehabilitation houses
For those who, despite their wishes and efforts, cannot sustain drug-freeness while living in the community, the option of referral to a residential rehabilitation house should be considered. Some five hundred places are available at such houses distributed among about twenty houses run by non-statutory organizations. The expected length of stay varies between one and two years. The content of programmes varies, but houses can be divided into three broad categories.

1. *Concept based therapeutic communities:* this is the largest and most cohesive group. All stem ultimately from the American Synanon model, but the details of their functioning have been extensively modified over the years to suit local conditions. Houses in this category include Alpha House, Suffolk House, the Ley Community, Inward House and the various Phoenix Houses. Staffed by a mixture of qualified professionals and ex-addicts who have been through the same or a similar programme, they all possess a hierarchical structure into which the new resident enters at the bottom. Typically, the newcomer is assigned to one of a number of work teams (kitchen, garden, house maintenance, etc.) under the management of a senior resident. Residents are expected to obey orders and act 'as if' they were responsible individuals in control of their feelings and behaviour. Behaviour and attitudes will determine promotion within the hierarchy, success bringing with it increased power and responsibility and fresh challenges. Residents may be demoted at any point if they are performing unsatisfactorily, or if it is felt that this would be a positive learning experience for them. To balance and interact with this rigid regimen, great use is made of a variety of group techniques – encounter, gestalt, psycho-drama, sensitivity and other methods associated with growth psychology. During group meetings, the emotional constraints and hierarchy are abandoned and residents are expected and encouraged to confront each other and staff in as honest a way as possible. Staff and residents act together to challenge anti-social and destructive behaviour and to reinforce positive ways of relating to self and others. Residents are encouraged to develop a new self-image and abilities and to leave behind their old drug-using persona and coping strategies. As they progress, the tight bonds of the programme are progressively relaxed until, in the 're-entry phase', they are expected to make preparations for leaving by spending more time outside the house, finding employment or signing up for an educational or training course. On completion of the programme, the resident becomes a 'graduate' of the house.

2. *Christian-based houses:* these include the Life for the World Trust, Teen Challenge, the Coke Hole Trust, Yeldall Manor and Deliverance International. A more disparate group than the concept-based houses, their distinguishing feature is the role that Christianity plays, always as a source of staff motivation and usually, in varying degrees, as an element in the therapeutic programme. Such houses tend to see problem drug use as having, in addition to physical, psychological and social components, a spiritual dimension as well. To a greater or lesser extent, they emphasize the role of bible study and Christian thought as an integral part of their therapeutic approach. In some cases it is a minor component, in others it dominates the programme. Conversion is not seen as a necessary precon-

dition of successful rehabilitation, but in some houses the philosophy tends to encourage it. In contrast to the intensity of the concept-based therapeutic communities, Christian houses can be seen as substitute families, earthly and spiritual, and as somewhere to seek refuge from a chaotic world. Support and counselling and sometimes group work are included in their programmes, as is work in the house and grounds. Contacts with outside Christian groups and individuals are strong, a considerable advantage allowing placement and support for residents at the end of their stay.

3. *Community-based houses:* a very varied category, defined more by its heterogeneity than anything else, but whose members seek in various ways to build links with their local communities and use local resources to the benefit of residents. The Elizabeth House Association houses are comprised, not only of staff and ex-drug user residents, but also of a group made up of people who work in a variety of outside occupations. This is intended to dilute the importance that past drug use assumes in the life of the house. The various houses run by Cranstoun Projects use more formal approaches of counselling and group work, but at a less intense level than do the concept-based communities, and use local resources to provide opportunities for education, leisure activities and work. The Richmond Fellowship's Crescent House is patterned on the democratic therapeutic community model pioneered by Maxwell Jones.

Other residential facilities
The ROMA project in London is a residential facility which does not require residents to be drug-free. It accepts residents who are receiving an opiate prescription from a clinic or general practitioner and aims to assist in stabilizing drug use, and to improve personal and social functioning, encouraging and supporting residents to obtain education, work and accommodation. Abstinence is encouraged, but is not seen as the primary or only goal. Many residents do stop using drugs and are referred on to one of the drug-free programmes discussed above.

City Roads Crisis Intervention Unit, also in London, started life in response to the chaotic barbiturate use rife during the mid-1970s (Jamieson, Glanz and MacGregor 1984). It has since broadened its scope to accommodate opiate users. Its brief is to accept users in a state of drug-related crisis. The three-week programme provides fast detoxification from opiates and barbiturates, combined with one-to-one counselling. Staffed by a mixture of social workers and nurses, its aim is to provide an environment where people in crisis can recuperate physically and receive help to review their situation and make plans for change, such as opting for residential rehabilitation. As would be expected from the nature of the client group, many need to go through the programme on more than one occasion before they can sustain their commitment to change.

Despite their widely-differing approaches, all types of residential re-habilitation houses seem to enjoy roughly the same degree of success, although research is sadly lacking in this area. The presence of such diversity is welcome: it mirrors the diversity of problem drug takers themselves. Individuals who find one regime insupportable may flourish in another. Social workers should familiarize themselves with the details of the various alternatives when considering a referral and go through them with the client, rather than making an arbitrary decision or pressing the claims of the regime which seems most attractive to them. Unfortunately, in practice it is not always possible to fit the right client to the ideal house, since the demand for places is high and waiting lists can build up. Funding for rehabilitation places is largely covered by DHSS payments, but houses will expect the residue to be provided from social services funds. This can prove difficult, as local authorities vary in their willingness to meet these charges.

Private sector
Rehabilitation is also provided in residential programmes run by private medical companies or charitable trusts registered as nursing homes. These charge fees directly to the resident, although 'assisted places', part-funded by DHSS social security payments are available. Many of these facilities employ the so-called 'Minnesota Model' (Wells 1987). This holds that there is a specific disease of 'chemical dependency'; that total abstinence from all psychoactive drugs including alcohol is necessary for recovery; and that adherence to the principles of Narcotics Anonymous will lead to recovery. In-patient treatment lasts for six to eight weeks. Following discharge, regular attendance at NA meetings is expected and encouraged. Those who have successfully achieved and sustained abstinence are not seen as 'cured', but as 'recovering addicts', in exactly the same way that Alcoholics Anonymous sees its members as 'recovering alcoholics'. It perhaps needs to be emphasized that Narcotics Anonymous, although often closely linked in practice with private-sector rehabilitation services, does not itself accept payment or funding from any source.

Some doctors in private practice prescribe to drug takers.

Advice and support to workers
There are several resources which can be useful to social workers dealing with drug-related issues. Several areas including the South West, Mersey-side, Cheshire and the North West are now served by training and informa-tion centres. Apart from training they can provide background information, advice on responding to individual cases and assistance in developing guidelines for good practice. All district health authorities should have es-tablished drug advisory committees as the result of a governmental circular. While they may vary in their depth of knowledge, they ought to be able to

offer some advice, at least on local services. Some health and/or local authorities have appointed drug misuse officers to assess needs, support policy and practice developments and coordinate activities.

There are several national bodies concerned with drug-related issues. Release, which provides information and advice on legal and drug-related problems, has over the years established a wide reputation for its expertise in the field of drugs and the law. The Terence Higgins Trust can provide extensive information on the facts and issues surrounding AIDS. The Institute for the Study of Drug Dependence has a comprehensive library of books and journals dealing with drug matters and publishes much useful material. The Standing Conference on Drug Abuse, the national coordinating body for non-statutory drug projects, is a valuable source of advice and has comprehensive contacts with drug services in England and Wales. Its publications include a regular newsletter, a detailed directory of rehabilitation services and a comprehensive guide to all drug services in Great Britain.

7 Recognizing Drug Use

Introduction

Until recently, most social workers did not count many known drug users amongst their case loads. Area teams, day-care facilities and residential units are often overstretched, and difficult decisions have to be made about priorities and the apportioning of resources to particular client groups. A number of factors have influenced the low priority given to work with drug-using clients. These include: the image of drug takers as undeserving of or not wanting help; the low representation of drug takers amongst those groups for whom social services have a statutory responsibility in most parts of the country; the unwillingness of many users to approach social services departments; beliefs on the part of workers that drug users are a medical responsibility; and a lack of clarity and confidence about the role that generic social workers might adopt. However, a greater understanding of problems related to the long-term use of minor tranquillizers, and the more widespread use of licit and illicit drugs for recreational purposes, have led to an increase of potential and actual problem drug use by clients referred to social services for other reasons, and an increase in those referred directly because of their drug use. At the same time, current social policies, reflected in the large number of new social work posts created specifically to work with drug users, clearly recognize that social workers can make a considerable contribution to the development and provision of a coordinated multi-disciplinary response to problem drug use.

Social workers in many settings are excellently placed to work with problem drug takers and their families and have the basic skills to assess and intervene. But many understandably feel insecure in this area: ignorant of specialist information; unsure of how to ascertain and interpret data; lacking in confidence and expertise; and isolated in their work. Furthermore, whilst trying to avoid stereotypes it cannot be denied that some drug takers are difficult to deal with, can be very demanding, may have complex problems, and that prior experience of working with them, or support from someone who has, can be very reassuring.

There are a range of skills, frameworks and models available for the assessment of problem drug use and the development of helping strategies. The social worker will already possess many of these skills and some of the methods, often to an advanced level. Skills in casework, assessment, developing a trusting and productive relationship and counselling, can be as appropriate to drug takers as they are to other client groups.

Recognition

Clients seen by staff of specialist drug agencies will usually have come because of the existence of some drug-related problem or other which they freely acknowledge. Their use of drugs is, as it were, their ticket into the service. Workers in other settings, however, may be faced with clients either unaware of the contribution that drug use is making to their problems, or unwilling to admit to drug use at all.

There will be cases where it is obvious to the social worker that the client is heavily involved in drug use as evidenced by their behaviour, appearance and the fact that they are clearly intoxicated at every meeting. Some clients will approximate the stereotype of 'the drug taker', but very many will not.

Drug takers cannot be identified with the aid of a simple check list. Many do not appear obviously intoxicated even when under the influence of the drug. Others may be in control of their drug use, confining it to recreational situations and always presenting to the social worker in a drug-free state. There are times when even experienced workers are unsure as to whether a client has returned to using after a period of abstinence, creating an impasse in the relationship which can only be resolved by frankness between worker and client. When one remembers that young people living in the family home can take heroin for many months before their actions come to the attention of their parents, and that many people report that they are ignorant of their partner's drug use over a period of years (some never find out about it), it is not surprising that a social worker may not detect drug use in the space of six interviews, let alone an initial assessment.

Many of the so-called 'signs and symptoms of drug use' can be attributable to other causes: to food allergies (bad coordination, hyperactivity); adolescent behaviour (poor concentration, mood swings, secrecy); to anxiety, depression, or any number of physical factors. Furthermore, physiological and behavioural effects vary with drug, dosage, degree of intoxication and a host of other factors. Pin-point pupils are often cited as a certain indicator of addiction but apart from the impracticality of staring myopically into the eyes of a client – especially if dark glasses, another commonly cited indicator, are being worn – only certain drugs, notably the opiates, give rise to pin-point pupils. Amphetamines would have the opposite effect.

Physical signs should not be dismissed altogether, but neither should they be relied on absolutely if they are not drug-specific. In addition it can be helpful to consider possible psychological, behavioural and environmental indicators. Again it is important not to place undue emphasis on any of these, as they may be unrelated to drug use. One should cross-check where possible, making use of all the available facts. If a client appears hyperactive, agitated or paranoid, this could be indicative of amphetamine use. But is there any other evidence to support this conclusion? For example, has the client lost weight? Is this drug known to be available in the area? Is the client likely to have access to it? Or might the behaviour have a totally different root? Perhaps the client is emotionally distressed or experiencing psychological problems unrelated to drug use.

Workers have been known to dismiss the idea of asking clients if they are using drugs, on the basis that they will automatically deny it. Whether or not this is so in any given case, such diffidence can have unfortunate implications for the relationship. Clients may assume that the worker is frightened to confront the drug use, or is totally unaware of it. As a result, some may feel unsafe about raising the topic themselves, anticipating that they will be met with an unhelpful response. Others may conclude that they can manipulate the situation to their own advantage, and yet others will be made to feel even more ashamed of their drug use and so unable to discuss it without prompting. By not asking the client, workers deprive themselves of the simplest way of finding out if someone is using.

Case example: Sharon, aged 15

Sharon was placed on a supervision order following a spate of shoplifting carried out in the company of a small group of 15-year-olds. Although intelligent, with a promising early school record, she had been truanting for almost a year. She was charming, attractive and impeccably dressed. Although she did not see the relevance of many of the discussions held with the social worker and was scathing about her school and the court's actions, she usually attended appointments and was increasingly willing to take an active part in them. The worker focussed on her changed behaviour assuming it to be related to her personal growth and development, to her need for a group identity and independence from her parents.

Drug use was not considered until one of Sharon's peers was arrested for possession of heroin. At about the same time a group of local workers started to collate information about the nature and extent of drug use in the area and it soon became apparent that it was more prevalent than had been realized. In view of this, the social worker began to consider a possible connection between Sharon's shoplifting and drug use. The social worker used a supervision session to confront her own anxieties and attitudes, aware that her picture of a drug taker did not include someone like Sharon. The worker also undertook research on the effects of drugs known to be available in the local area.

In the absence of any other supporting indicators, the worker kept an open mind and felt it inappropriate to adopt a confrontative approach in the first instance, as this might destroy any trust that had developed. Rather, she asked Sharon for her opinions on the recent reports that the estate where she lived was 'awash with heroin'. In the context of an interested but non-judgemental and relatively casual conversation, she was able to ask Sharon if she had taken drugs. An affirmative answer was not immediately taken as evidence of *problem* drug use.

*

If Sharon had denied taking drugs, the worker should have relied on her instinct and knowledge of the case, taking into account how Sharon had responded to the question and any subsequent difficulties in their relationship, and, if appropriate, raised the matter again in the light of any further pointers. While always retaining a caring and non-judgemental approach, it might have become necessary to be more directive if the worker believed that the sessions were unproductive because drug use was being deliberately avoided as a relevant concern. There are cases where a more confrontative approach is essential: where, for example, the worker believes the client or someone close to them is at serious risk; where an urgent assessment is necessary; or where statemate has been reached and movement can only be achieved through an exploration of drug use. It should be noted, though, that difficulties between worker and client can arise, not because the latter is denying drug use, but because the former cannot move away from the possibility which, although unspoken, still conveys itself to the client.

In this instance, the worker made very real plans before the session. She accepted the need to confront her own preconceptions which had not allowed for the possibility that Sharon could be involved in drug use, increased her confidence by gathering factual information, which also proved reassuring to Sharon, and ensured that professional support and guidance would be provided. Preliminary planning also meant that the worker did not make the mistake of assuming that Sharon was shoplifting to finance her drug use simply because of the new evidence about local patterns of use. It became something to check out and to consider or eliminate as appropriate. She was thus able to confront Sharon in an informed way without being threatening or judgemental. Aware that she would not have considered drug use if it had not been for external factors, the worker accepted the need to reappraise her ideas of recognition, the importance of keeping abreast of local patterns of drug use, and of cross-checking a variety of pointers in working with Sharon and other clients. She was able to rely on the strength of the relationship and Sharon's personality.

Possible indicators of drug use

Some possible indicators of drug use are set out below. Any such list should be employed with the greatest caution. With few exceptions, the indicators can be attributable to other causes and not diagnostic of drug use at all, let alone of problematic use. Workers should familiarize themselves with the effects of commonly used drugs, as this information will suggest possible points to bear in mind.

Physical
Injection sites, or 'track marks' (the marks left by injecting).

Client looks or behaves intoxicated or 'stoned'.
Client 'nods off'.
Poor coordination.
Eyes – red, watery, over-bright or dull, staring, heavy, vacant.
Appears generally ill or drawn.
Poor complexion and skin complaints.
Weight loss. Physical deterioration.
Wasted muscles.
Swollen and damaged hands.
Apparent loss of interest in appearance.

Behavioural
Mood swings, inappropriate or unpredictable behaviour.
Excessive responses.
Depressed, lethargic, relaxed, irritable, edgy, agitated.
Happy, content.
Hopeless and helpless, adopting 'victim personality'.
Lack of concentration and interest.
Fatigue.
Withdrawn.
Frightened, paranoid.
Absenteeism, lack of punctuality – work and school.
Deterioration of work or school record, or home life.
Deterioration of relationships and social skills.

General factors
Evidence of the substance or method of use, e.g. glue, burn marks or
    blood on clothes, burnt tin foil, syringes.
What are the local patterns of drug use?
Who do they mix with? Where do they live?
Are they becoming more involved in criminal activities?

8 Developing the Relationship: Understanding the Problem Drug Taker

The client/worker relationship is open to a host of influences which may be detrimental or helpful both to the initial interview and to subsequent interactions. If steps are taken from the outset to engender a constructive relationship it will be possible to avoid some of the potential stumbling blocks. The following paragraphs explore some of the relevant issues, such as: the worker's attitudes and expectations; how the client might feel about the interview; trust; the pitfalls of talking about drugs; denial and exaggeration of drug use; whether to work with someone if they are under the influence of a drug, aggressive or unpredictable behaviour.

1. The worker's attitudes

We are all drug takers, all dependent on something, whether it be a substance (cigarettes, coffee, food), a relationship, or a favourite hobby or pastime. This should be remembered when working with clients who are drug takers. They are not an alien species. As noted in Chapter 5, the reasons for using socially disapproved drugs overlap to a large extent with the reasons why all of us use socially approved ones. Unproblematic drug use is typified by lack of legal or economic constraints, by context, and by the fact that users have other means of achieving the same ends, or are not unduly agitated if their drug is not available to them. Such unproblematic use may be common to worker and client, but even if the latter is experiencing difficulties, the social worker should recognize the existence of a continuum and recall the very relative nature of drug use and dependence.

Chapter 2 discussed the strongly-held attitudes which surround drugs and drug takers and stressed the importance of reflecting upon whether one's own beliefs and attitudes have negative implications for response. It is not helpful to initiate an assessment from a moralistic, patronizing, evangelistic or stereotypically informed basis. It does not bode well if clients feel that the worker disapproves of them perhaps to the point of indifference, is sorry for them, or wants to change their lives dramatically in accordance with the worker's own values and expectations. How a worker feels about a drug, or about the person taking that drug, will affect the quality of service that the client receives. If the drug is seen as dangerous and unacceptable, then the drug taker may be similarly labelled. If workers hold stereotypes based on sex, age, race and cultural background, their assessments of drug use and related problem areas will be affected by the interface of the two sets of misapprehensions or caricatures. Thus a 19-year-old working-class man may be more likely to be suspected of heroin use than a 30-year-old middle-class woman; a group of unemployed black teenagers may be more likely to rouse suspicions of cannabis use in the worker's mind than would a group of young white professionals who meet socially. Received but mistaken wisdom and unfounded assumptions can have far-reaching implications. Cannabis provides an example of a drug that can elicit quite divergent responses from workers, regardless of the needs and circumstances of the individual client.

Case example: John
John was accepted at an Intermediate Treatment Centre following disruptive behaviour, truanting and minor theft. In the course of an informal group discussion, he mentioned that he regularly smoked cannabis. One staff member was appalled, convinced that his behaviour resulted directly from his drug use which in turn would certainly lead on to the injection of heroin and the mortuary slab. The worker strongly argued for referral to a drug dependence unit and police involvement. Another worker, who had personal experience of the drug, was adamant that John would not experience difficulties as a result of smoking cannabis and that his revelation should go unchallenged.

*

Here, neither worker was considering the specifics of John's situation. Both were reacting from their own experience and attitudes. Not only might John's actual needs have gone unmet, but lack of coherent agency policy or commitment to it could have resulted in friction amongst workers and with attenders.

Clients may be categorized as problem drug takers when they are not and so have to contend with problems arising from an inappropriate and loaded label. Just as seriously, clients may seek help with their drug use but be advised that there is no problem, without any meaningful assessment being made, or any credence given to the clients' perceptions of their own situations. Past experience of drug use and of working with drug takers can be of great help, but not if it merely serves to create absolutist assumptions from which the client cannot escape. Assessment and helping strategy must revolve around the circumstances of the individual.

2. How the client feels about the interview
It is worthwhile considering how the client may be feeling about the interview. Clients may be angry that they have been referred at all, feel betrayed by someone to whom they are close, suspicious of the purpose of the interview, or scared that they have reached the point where they have finally to face up to a problem. It is sometimes useful to discuss these matters

with clients. Any statutory responsibility should be explained, as clients may be more amenable if they can see a clear purpose to the assessment which does not preclude the possibility that their drug use may be not problematic and that, if a problem does exist, the worker is prepared to explore options for help sympathetically. Measures should be taken to make the client feel welcome and safe in an emotional and practical sense. Will the interview be overheard or interrupted? Do certain records have to be taken and, if so, why? Are drug takers apparently or actually seen in the least comfortable part of the premises? Again some of these points should be raised, as doing so can help to acknowledge and/or appease anxieties.

It is understandable that some drug takers will feel hesitant in being open about their drug-taking and associated behaviour. Many feel ashamed or embarrassed, wary that the worker will be openly disapproving, so further reducing their self-esteem. They may have suffered a series of painful rejections because of their drug use and have no guarantee that they will be accepted this time. Workers may have strong feelings about how they expect a drug taker to behave – for example that such clients will be untruthful, manipulative, aggressive, intoxicated or unmotivated – or believe on principle that clients should simply stop using. They may lack confidence, feel ignorant of the facts of drug-induced experiences, or be unnerved by their apparent powerlessness to interrupt the client's chaotic and life-threatening behaviour. Any of this may be communicated to clients and leave them in turn feeling unsafe and reluctant to discuss their lives.

Clients may not be prepared to discuss certain areas because they are fearful about what the worker may do with the information. Will it be passed on to the police, partners or parents? If they are open about their drug use, will it have devastating consequences on their lives? For example, might their children be taken into care, or might clients be evicted because they have contravened the rules of the hostel where they are living? Trust is essential: establishing and maintaining it is particularly important with a client group whose drug-using activities are at the very least likely to be frowned upon and often involve breaches of the law.

The issue of confidentiality is inextricably bound up with trust and care should be taken to ensure that clients are informed of exactly what is meant by it in the setting of the agency and of the circumstances in which information might be passed to outsiders. There are no easy answers to the question of confidentiality, but so long as the client knows the ground rules, the worker is less likely to break confidentiality and thus destroy any element of trust that might have been established.

Case example: Mark
Mark was very distressed to discover that his social worker had informed his parents that he was using drugs. Until then he had been forthcoming in

sessions, but any degree of trust and safety was lost because the worker 'went behind my back'.

*

It is useful to explain early on in the relationship the kind of information that might have to be passed on, and why. Reasons might arise from statutory obligations or from concern that the client or someone close to them is at risk. Whilst clients may welcome an onward referral, they are often unaware of the extent of detailed information which is passed on, usually to fulfil the required referral procedure. Workers should inform clients about the nature of the information exchange wherever possible, should be clear in their own minds that they are relaying only pertinent information, and should clarify why cooperation with a third party might ultimately be in the client's interest. It is also helpful to be able to assure clients that wherever possible, information will only be passed on with their knowledge, preferably after discussion. Most importantly, clients should be encouraged to divulge necessary information themselves. Problems may arise when a worker has knowledge of an assessment on a client to which the client is not permitted access.

In the example above, Mark's social worker should have explained that his parents suspected he was using drugs and were very anxious, wanting to respond in the most helpful way. If Mark had been able to reveal the facts himself it might have improved his relationship with his parents who would then have been in a better position to help him. The worker could have helped Mark to practise telling his parents, and discussed what could happen after their suspicions were confirmed. Mark might have welcomed the intervention of the social worker, either while he was present or not. The worker could have adopted a more advocative and supportive role, rather than an apparently authoritarian one.

3. Talking about drugs

(a) Why focus on drugs?

An admission or evidence that a client is taking drugs may suggest that a more thorough examination of the nature and extent of use would be helpful in establishing patterns of behaviour and related areas of concern for the client and others. If it is felt necessary to take a drug history, the worker should decide whether it needs to be detailed and complex or whether a simple account will suffice. A drug history may be relevant if it is pertinent to the referral, or is necessary in compiling a report for a court, or for onward referral. Once the possibility emerges that drug use may be a factor in a case, workers sometimes become fixated upon this. The fact that drug use may be suspected or even confirmed should not lead the social worker to conclude that there must necessarily be a related problem, and should not detract from investigation of other areas of the client's life, or become the sole focus of enquiry. (See Chapter 9 on assessment.) Workers should always be clear about the purpose of discussing drug use at any given moment.

Some clients, particularly if they feel confident in an addict identity, or if they present with a drug problem, may be eager to concentrate on their drug use from the first interview. Others will eventually feel safe and look forward to discussing their drug use with someone who is drug-free and non-judgemental. The worker must ensure that this emphasis is relevant and used constructively and be wary of inadvertently reinforcing an addict or victim identity as this will be a further hurdle to the client attempting change. Some clients may feel that they have to behave in a certain way to fulfil this role, knowing that they will achieve a response. The worker should aim to show that it is the person that they are primarily interested in, not the drug.

Drug takers can be charming and entertaining, and workers may find themselves tacitly encouraging more anecdotes than are strictly necessary for getting to know the client, establishing rapport or clarifying the significance of drugs in the client's life. This interest may verge on voyeurism or collusion. The reason for the relationship can be lost, making it difficult to confront other issues or to return to a more formal basis. It can be tempting for a social worker who is unprepared and at a loss as to how to proceed with the interview to resort to discussing drug use. If a worker does feel 'stuck' it is far better to take the case to supervision if possible and appropriate, and to look for alternative openings and approaches with the client, than to shirk the problem by doing the only thing that makes immediate sense — that is, to focus on drugs. The chances are that the client will be aware that the worker does not know what to do and will react accordingly. The client's problems may be variously hidden, exacerbated or created by drug use, or indeed be unrelated to it. Any focus on drug-taking should be aimed at clarifying why and where problems exist, and the role that drugs play in creating or coping with them. If sessions continually dwell on drug use, workers should ask themselves if the information obtained is pertinent and the focus valid.

When approaching a painful or difficult stage in assessment or counselling, clients may revert to talking about their drug use because it is now a relatively comfortable area for them. A similar retreat into drug-centred talk may occur after a client has confronted a difficult topic and feels a need to relax before venturing deeper. There is some worth in allowing these safe plateaux, where clients can as it were re-muster their forces, but it should be recognized that if over-indulged, such episodes can be an effective avoidance technique.

If clients, rightly or wrongly do not consider that they have a drug problem, they may dismiss any discussion of drug use as irrelevant and a waste of time. The worker should explain the reasons for pursuing this line of enquiry and accept that clients may be correct in their interpretation of the situation.

There are other reasons why users will claim to view talking – not just about drugs, but globally – as irrelevant. Counselling and related approaches, relying as they do on the articulation of feeling and the more or less sophisticated use of language, are not techniques immediately attractive to all clients. They often conflict with cultural norms and are alien means of problem-solving for many groups. It is not easy to express emotional pain and confusion under such circumstances. For drug takers whose self-esteem is destroyed, the process may appear especially intimidating. Many other clients have not reached the emotional maturity to take strength from a counselling relationship. If they conceptualize their problem as being solely one of 'physical addiction', they will see the solution in terms of medical treatment, a 'cure', something which is done to them and which they passively receive. They may see no need for themselves to be involved in a two-way process. Bearing these points in mind, workers should aim to provide a safe environment for the client to discuss his or her drug use, accepting that there will be times when their services will not be acceptable to or usable by the client. Eventually, many clients experience an incredible sense of relief that they can at last talk about their drug use openly.

Case example: Marge
At the age of sixteen, Marge sought a referral to a Drug Dependence Unit for detoxification from heroin. She refused all offers of out-patient support. She soon returned to drug use and underwent a series of detoxifications over a period of eighteen months. Only after this time did she admit the need for something more than help with the physical pain of withdrawal. 'I can cope with clucking [withdrawal]. But I can't stand what it's doing to my head and my heart. It's all in here.'

*

(b) Denial and exaggeration
Many workers embark on a drug history with a sincere belief that the client will be manipulative and deliberately untruthful. It is true that drug takers may withhold or distort information, but there are reasons for this which need to be explored before the client is condemned out of hand. In 'Dealing With Drink' Davies and Raistrick state: 'given the opportunity problem drinkers are much more honest than is often believed.' (Davies and Raistrick 1981). Given the right circumstances and encouragement, this is also true of problem drug takers. It would be helpful to both client and worker if this premise could be more widely accepted.

It is not unusual for a client to over- or underestimate the amount and frequency of his drug use. Most people would find it hard to remember exactly how much tea or alcohol they drank, or how many television programmes they watched over the previous week. It is hardly surprising then that problem drug takers often have only a vague idea how much heroin they have taken over some months or years. The drug, life-style, and lack of practice in establishing clear patterns conspire to produce a confused and unrealistic picture. With prompting, time and tools such as keeping a diary (see Chapter 10), a clearer picture can emerge and the client is often surprised that he has miscalculated to such a degree.

Drug takers develop survival skills, and denial and rationalization may be amongst them. These can arise out of fear of rejection, shame, or an unwillingness to confront a drug problem. Denial is not just a way of misleading the worker, but of protecting the drug taker from a frightening and unacceptable reality. To admit to the extent to which they resort to drugs to escape from or deal with problems, may ultimately deprive them of their only means of coping. In time they may come to believe some of the little lies that they have been telling in order to maintain any degree of self-worth.

It is not uncommon, on the other hand, for people to boast about their drug use. They may be looking for credibility, establishing an identity, or trying to show that they are good at something – even if it is at being an addict. Rather more negatively, some may be so insecure and desperate that they believe that they have to exaggerate the seriousness of their circumstances in order to get any help, while others may be trying to get the worker to reject them.

(c) Jargon

The world of illicit drug-taking has its own rich store of jargon words and phrases which may both baffle and attract the outsider. Workers tempted to employ slang terms with their clients should reflect that the use of jargon can be a double-edged sword. It can be a way of establishing empathy with clients, of showing that you know what they are talking about. It can also be a form of shorthand when trying to establish drug use in an emergency when the client is heavily intoxicated. On the other hand, workers should not be tempted to over-identify with their clients. And if a worker uses jargon inappropriately, whether by using obsolete words from their own past, or by misapplying contemporary phrases, they may lose credibility with the client. Jargon changes from time to time, place to place and may even be used differently on neighbouring estates. It follows that workers should only use jargon if they are really comfortable with it and clear about its application. If workers are unclear about the meaning of drug jargon used by their clients, then it is far better to ask than to pretend a knowledge they do not posses.

Furthermore, the worker may neglect an essential health education role by using slang. Drug takers themselves may not be aware that a familiar jargon term actually refers to a drug that has serious associated health risks. In 1982 a number of young people in South London were taking 'skag' unaware that it was heroin. Workers should always ensure that both they and the client know what drug the slang term refers to so that any necessary harm reduction information can be imparted.

4. Intoxication: how stoned is too stoned?

One too often encounters the view that there is no point in working with a client who is intoxicated. This position is too simplistic, and occasions will certainly arise when workers will find themselves responding to clients who are under the influence of drugs and will have to take a decision about the best way of handling the situation. Rather than drawing impractical distinctions between 'straight' and 'stoned', workers must recognize that 'intoxication' defines a spectrum of states, from almost sober to totally incapacitated , each of which offers differing opportunities for alternative styles of intervention.

On a purely practical level, it can be difficult to know if the client is intoxicated, as not all consequent behaviour is uncontrolled . Drug users, like drinkers, can often gauge their intake to achieve a semblence of normality and control, both for themselves and in the way that they present to the world at large. A client may take a drug just before an interview, appear perfectly lucid at first but gradually fall under the influence of the substance. Conversely, clients may choose to appear more intoxicated than they actually are because they do not want to engage in a session, or think such behaviour is expected of them. They may then sober up during the course of the interview. Opiate users who are receiving a legitimate methadone prescription and people prescribed minor tranquillizers will be more or less permanently under the influence of their drug to some degree.

There are other reasons why clients may present in an intoxicated condition. They may be unable or unwilling to come in a drug-free state, especially if they are dependent. To be drug-free may mean that they are experiencing withdrawals, and at best they will feel vulnerable. To a drug-dependent individual 'feeling normal' is associated with being under the influence of a drug, not with being drug-free. Given that the interview itself can be a stressful situation it is no wonder that clients may turn to their proven coping mechanism and take the drug beforehand. Since the very purpose of social work intervention may be to help them towards drug-freeness, to insist that clients achieve this state before any work is possible risks being seen as paradoxical.

There will be occasions when clients are very intoxicated and difficult to manage. Intoxicated behaviour can be intimidating, unfair to other clients and staff and disruptive to set programmes. It can be a waste of time for worker and client alike and, if unchallenged, the behaviour could be reinforced. It is often at this point that shortcomings in agency policy and training — for example, in procedures for dealing with overdoses or aggression — emerge. It is preferable to clarify these issues before the need arises to put procedures into practice.

Measures to deal with these management problems may actively conflict with the needs of the individual, so the worker should aim for a balance between the rights and needs of the particular client, other clients and staff. In extreme circumstances clients may have to be expelled or asked to leave immediately. Depending on their mood, it could be counterproductive to confront them about their behaviour at this stage and better to wait for a more appropriate and less emotive opportunity. At all stages it is important to convey the message that you are rejecting not them but their unacceptable behaviour. The worker should respond according to the circumstances, explaining why certain behaviour is unacceptable, clarifying the reasons behind this view and establishing the most appropriate response. Are clients trying to get the worker to reject them? Do they want more attention? Are they totally chaotic in their drug use and unable to exert any degree of control, or so desperate for help that they think that they have to exaggerate their problem in order to get help? Do they need somewhere safe to be 'stoned'? Are they simply being antagonistic?

Case example: Sandy
The staff at a day centre were very concerned about Sandy, who had a poor attendance record and was clearly often under the influence of heroin. While they acknowledged his drug problem, they did not confront his behaviour. No progress was made as staff were at pains not to threaten their precarious relationship with Sandy. When another drug taker called into the project, he was confronted in the presence of other clients. Sandy left the room and, when he returned, he had clearly taken more heroin, but was still not challenged. Following this episode, he did not attend the centre for several weeks. When asked about his absence, he retorted that he had felt that the staff did not care because they had not confronted him. He wanted rules, someone to say 'no' and share the responsibility of having to change his behaviour.

*

Case example: Mel
Mel came to reception asking to see her social worker. She was clearly distressed and intoxicated. She had been physically abused and as a result had taken a variety of drugs. The fact that she had resorted to this means of coping added to her distress and her self-image took two severe blows. She needed to be with someone she trusted.

*

Case example: Jane
Jane regularly turned up at the area team office in an intoxicated state and was intimidating to others. She was highly insistent in her demands which were usually the result of a whim. Her social worker rarely saw her on these occasions, but spent some time when Jane did keep appointments explaining why her behaviour ultimately proved to be self-defeating.

*

Clarity about the type of work that can be undertaken with someone who is intoxicated is essential. The degree and frequency with which the client is under the influence of a substance will affect the type of work that can seriously be undertaken. There is no point in attempting psychodynamic approaches when the client is barely capable of response. The worker has to use intuition and judgement over whether drug-induced revelations are maudlin or cathartic, or what to do when a client will only admit to problems when intoxicated (this raises interesting ethical questions about confidentiality and what right a worker has to such disclosures). Establishing a trusting relationship and working on harm reduction lines are likely to be more appropriate goals than total and immediate abstinence. Ground rules should be negotiated and clarified with the client, contracts used appropriately, and penalties, along with their implications, considered. This is not always easy, as what is unacceptable behaviour to the agency may be perfectly reasonable from the user's point of view. If penalties are applied then the relationship may suffer, perhaps permanently. The client may feel rejected and be unwilling to make use of the agency again. Certain restrictions, such as a life ban, deny the possibility of change unless coupled with an appropriate onward referral.

Workers may find it difficult to ask people to leave as they feel responsible for clients at risk due to their level of intoxication and chaotic actions. If policy allows, it is legitimate for the agency to function as a safe haven until the client is 'straight' enough to venture outside.

At times, there may seem no alternative but to call the police, in which case the client should if possible be informed of this decision, as he or she may then leave of their own accord. Above all, clients should be dealt with on as individual a basis as the policy of the agency allows, and workers should try to reach a balance of needs and be willing to be assertive when having to contend with a difficult client.

5. Aggression and unpredictable behaviour
Much of the preceding discussion on intoxication is equally pertinent to a consideration of aggressive and unpredictable behaviour.

Drug users have an undeserved reputation for being aggressive. Concern is often expressed that a drug-taking client will be physically violent because of the disinhibiting effects of drugs such as the barbiturates, or as a result of a paranoid reaction arising from amphetamine use. Such episodes are uncommon, but do occasionally occur. More pertinently, drug takers, like other clients, may sometimes be threatening for reasons other than the effects of intoxication. In certain situations they may feel hostile because the worker is attempting to carry out a statutory duty. Or they may be aggressive because of a sense of failure, desperation, internal conflict, or a general anger with the world or the worker, because despite seeking help they are not being offered immediate solutions either to their long-term problems or to their immediate needs, such as a bed for the night or a supply of drugs.

Apart from occasional unpredictable reactions attributable to the effect of the drug, drug users are no more likely to be violent or difficult to handle than other clients. Like them, their aggression more often manifests itself verbally. Admittedly, this in itself can be unpleasant and intimidating for workers. As a matter of general policy, services should establish strategies, including in-service training, to help staff to deal with potentially violent situations, minimize risk, and provide the most helpful possible response to the client.

Satisfactory procedures for dealing with the general problem will suffice for drug takers. The most important point is to move away from the stereotype that drug takers will inevitably be violent and abusive. Workers should not anticipate such behaviour without good reason, as this could help precipitate the very actions they are trying to avoid.

6. Overdose

The possibility of overdose leading to unconsciousness was briefly mentioned in the discussion of intoxication. Workers are unlikely to experience many such occurrences unless they are employed in specialist facilities, where standard procedures will be in operation, and even in such settings they are rather uncommon. Detailed procedures for coping with overdose cases would be inappropriate in a book of this nature. Normal first-aid measures should be applied and in all cases where an actual or suspected overdose is encountered, it is best to call an ambulance or other qualified medical help immediately.

9 Assessment

Purpose of assessment

The purpose, focus, and nature of the assessment process will be shaped to some extent by the reason for and source of the referral, and by whether drug use is a known, suspected or unconsidered factor. Nevertheless the general aim will be to establish a clear picture of the client's life and the role that drug use plays in it, to identify areas of difficulty and achievement and to explore related factors. Above all, a good assessment will enable client and worker to develop helping strategies and mechanisms for change with the maximum chance of a successful outcome which includes the client having greater control over his or her life. Conducted well, the assessment can help build the relationship between client and worker.

Social work literature generally points to the need to focus on two broad levels of enquiry and their interrelationship. Assessment should reveal information about the individual and that person's environment. Worker and client need to identify what problems are present in these two spheres and determine how existing personal strengths and environmental resources can be used or developed to bring about change. If the principles of good social work practice are adhered to, the social worker should be able to provide effective help to problem drug takers. The following sections make suggestions as to how the global term 'drug problem' can be more clearly understood and appropriate helping strategies identified.

The nature of the problem

The assessment process should clarify the following questions for both client and worker: Is there a problem? Is there a drug problem? Who is it a problem for? These questions can be difficult to separate out and the answers should not be assumed or taken for granted. Not only the worker's attitudes, but those of the referrer, the family, and the client will influence them, as will any number of other pressures. At this point, as elsewhere, the worker should aim for a dialogue with the client about their respective perceptions and interpretations and give due credence to the client's viewpoint. There may be a disagreement, but the ground will have been laid for a basic understanding from which to negotiate and proceed.

Case example: Jenny
Jenny was always incapacitated when seen by the social worker, in a poor state of health, regularly overdosing and with serious abscesses. The worker

responded to the very apparent drug problem. Sessions always deteriorated into an uncomfortable, sometimes hostile, impasse. In fact Jenny saw her drug use as a solution and the problem as one of homelessness and victimization. When the worker clarified, explored and responded to this, they were able to get out of the rut and discuss their differing perspectives. Shortcomings in Jenny's solution were identified, the stated problems dealt with practically (by referral to a hostel and other changes in the environment) and emotionally/psychologically (by examining why Jenny felt victimized), and more appropriate personal coping mechanisms and external resources explored.

*

Some clients may be referred solely or principally on the basis that they are drug takers. It does not automatically follow that drug use is either symptomatic or causative of problems. Nevertheless the worker could still have a role to play.

Case example: Jim

Jim's parents called the local police after finding pills in his bedroom. He was unwilling to discuss drugs with his family or the police, beyond insisting that he had only taken them occasionally and did not have a problem. He was subsequently referred to social services. The social worker spent some time creating a safe atmosphere, as it was clear that Jim was hurt and angry that his parents had called the police before talking to him. In time the assessment revealed that Jim was being truthful and that his drug use was very much under control. The social worker was certain that there was no drug problem but established two areas to work on:
(1) Jim's relationship with his parents. Why did the parents call the police as a first step? Was this indicative of real problems in the relationship? Was Jim's drug use the last straw in a spate of unacceptable behaviour? Was Jim being made a scapegoat as a way of the family avoiding other problems? If there were problems at home, was it possible that Jim would turn to drugs in the future as a means of escape? Even if the parents acted out of simple panic, what could be done to repair the relationship with Jim?
(2) Prevention. The worker adopted a secondary prevention approach in a bid to ensure that Jim's drug use did not escalate, clarifying with Jim the potential risks he might face, and providing appropriate health education.

*

In this case, the primary emphasis was taken from drug use, as the worker correctly decided that the problem was not a drug problem. At the same time, the opportunity was taken to impart information about possible future risks.

Case example: Fred

Following a long period of delinquent behaviour, Fred was admitted to an assessment centre. He regularly boasted to residents and staff about his drug taking and associated lifestyle. The staff noted that there were a number of discrepancies in his stories, that he was unable to talk about his experiences in any depth and, unlike other of the more 'up front' kids, he was irritating rather than amusing to his peers. Bearing this in mind, his drug use was ignored, except in formal sessions where he was asked quite directly but sympathetically if he really did take all the drugs that he boasted of. He eventually admitted that his drug experience was limited to one occasion when he had smoked cannabis. He wanted to be seen as a heavy drug taker in order to obtain some credibility with the others. There was no drug problem. Work was clearly necessary around the reasons for Fred's poor self-image and identity, and ways of improving it.

*

There are cases where, although drug use is not part of the presenting problem or contained in the referral information, it is still worth bearing the possibility in mind. Drugs, like alcohol, may be a hidden but causative factor. It is essential though that the possibility does not become the sole focus of enquiry.

Case example: Carol

Carol was fifteen, with four younger siblings. Over the previous twelve months her school attendance and performance, once above average, had become increasingly poor. She appeared run down, lost weight, and was withdrawn and moody. She was referred to education welfare. It was reasonable to consider that drug use might have played a role in her changed behaviour and appearance but there was no direct evidence. Her parents, aware of recent trends in drug use, insisted that the worker investigated this possibility. It would have been tempting to direct all focus on to possible drug use, but this could have been counterproductive given Carol's unwillingness to build a relationship. It seemed more appropriate to discuss with Carol if she felt she had changed, and if so why? Was she worried about the changes and the reasons for them? It transpired that she was confused about her sexuality and her role at home. She resented having to look after her brothers and sisters while her mother was at work or with her boyfriend. She was having to act as an adult, but had not had access to a growing-up process. The worker asked Carol if she ever took drugs to deal with her unhappiness and was satisfied when she replied that she had not. Thus there was a problem, but not a drug problem.

Case example: Joan
Joan sought help from social services. Her husband had left home and she hoped to find nursery places for her children. This would enable her to cope with them, and to seek work which would alleviate her isolation. Further discussion revealed that she felt depressed, listless and agitated in turn. Although she desperately wanted a job she was frightened of the prospect. Knowing that women in her position are often prescribed tranquillizers, the social worker asked if she had seen anyone else for help. Joan replied that she had seen her doctor. 'What did he do?' 'Gave me pills.' 'Are you happy with them?' 'No they make me feel weak and awful but I daren't stop.' The worker could have simply responded to the presenting problem and found a nursery for the children, or have left the assessment before exploring the possibility that Joan was on tranquillizers which may have ceased to be helpful and were now adding to her problems.

*

Often a person's drug use is pathologized when, in fact, it is a problem, not for the user, but for other people. This is a frequent reaction of users' relatives, courts and the public at large, and results from the attitudes towards drug use discussed in Chapter 2 . In such circumstances, it can be futile to respond to the using individual without dealing with others who are affected.

Case example: Ron and Jack
Ron and Jack were a long-established homosexual couple whose relationship was entering a state of crisis. Ron discovered that his lover had taken cocaine. Rather than admit that there might be difficulties within their relationship which needed to be faced and dealt with, he preferred to consider that Jack was dependent upon the drug and that all the problems stemmed from this.

*

This is also a strategy too often employed by staff in caring agencies, when the 'problem' is really one of staff attitudes and anxieties, poor management and lack of apposite policy. The staff feel unable to control the situation and resort to individual measures. For example, staff may respond to solvent users by transferring them, or by arranging formal counselling, or sessions with a child psychiatrist. While in some cases this might be appropriate, in

others it will definitely not be. Thought should be given to equipping staff
to deal more constructively with such situations. Modifications in policy
and programme, and provision of staff training, could result in a more
planned response which would take into account the needs of all concerned.

Information gathering
In some cases assessment will be on the basis of one interview, but where
a longer-term relationship exists the case will be continually reassessed and
a greater understanding achieved. Recognition, assessment, intervention
and rehabilitation will shade into one another. If there is a need for an
immediate assessment with no possibility for further discussion, then there
may well be inaccuracies and gaps simply because of the lack of time to
gather information and establish a trusting relationship. The worker should
aim to get as complete and relevant a picture as possible, and where there are
time constraints, should concentrate on those areas most pertinent to the immediate task – for example making an emergency referral or an assessment
for court or allocation.

Social workers will already have assessment and information-gathering
skills, and agencies possess an existing assessment procedure. Only two
modifications will be necessary in cases where drug use is a factor. First, the
information-gathering process will have to include current patterns of drug
use and, in a fuller assessment, a drug history may be called for. Secondly,
any interpretation of data should include the significance of drug use for
other aspects of the client's situation. The following points should be
covered in an assessment, though workers should use their initiative as to
whether some areas are more or less relevant, and the order in which they
should be addressed. It should be remembered that assessment is a *process*
and that the relative importance of different influences, cues and pressures
will often vary from day to day. It follows that this will affect both
motivation and suitable response.

Personal data
Drug takers are often wary about giving their name or address (if they have
one), lest information is passed on to the police or the Home Office. Social
workers should assure clients that they are not obliged to notify drug takers
to the Home Office, and in the event of having to pass on information
elsewhere, should explain the necessity for this. More often than not, the
client's name will be known from the referral information, but if it is not, and
is not formally required at this point, there is no harm in agreeing to use a
pseudonym. The age, sexuality, race and cultural background of a client
influence the kinds of problems that they may experience. Anonymous
monitoring of such data can provide useful material for developing a
meaningful equal opportunities policy, identifying gaps in service provision
and evolving tailored responses for particular client groups.

Presenting problem
Why was the client referred and by whom? How does the client view the referral and the situation? Do they identify a problem? Specifically, do they feel that they have a drug problem?

Current circumstances
The worker should gather general background information to the current situation and identify related areas of concern. These include, for example:

The type and security of accommodation; do they live alone or with
   a partner, family, friends, other users?
Relationships.
Financial situation.
Are they in work, unemployed, at college or at school?
General physical and psychological well-being.
Legal situation

Drug use
Current drug use. What drugs are they taking, how often and when? Are there any obvious patterns? What is the desired effect they seek from the drug? Are there any obvious problems related to drug use?

HIV / AIDS
Is the client at risk of contracting or spreading the HIV virus through patterns of drug use or sexual activity?

All these areas are pertinent to initial assessment and early onward referral. If the client identifies drug use as a problem, the interview may concentrate on this more than on other areas of the client's life, but these must be considered in the longer term if a fuller picture is necessary to the purpose of the relationship. All the above areas can be pursued and explored more coherently, devoting time to non-problem and problem areas, periods and instances of success and failure, happiness and unhappiness. How far the worker concentrates on history as opposed to the current situation and recent past, will depend on worker and agency style, but each case must be judged according to individual circumstances. Many drug takers have immediate problems and, at least initially, are not in an emotional or physical position to consider the effects of early experience on their current behaviour.

The relationship and significance of drug use to other factors needs to be clarified. A client may give different information on drug use from one session to another, for reasons outlined earlier. In time a clearer picture will emerge, particularly if the worker assists in the process.

Client and worker need to look at:

    Length of use .
    Occasions that give rise to use.
    Desired effect (in both the past and the present).
    Current patterns and style of use.
    Periods of heavy or chaotic use.
    Periods of stability or abstinence.
    What are the reasons for these?
    Why did the client resume drug use after a period of being drug-
        free?
    Does the client feel in control or have drugs become a problem?
    What sort of problems are emerging?
    Why and when did they first appear?
    How important is drug use to the client?
    Is it affecting other areas of the client's life?

The answers can indicate areas where changes might be desirable, and where problems might rest and be in need of examination.

10 Drug Takers as Parents

Although drug use is sometimes associated with decreased libido and reduced fertility, there are many reasons why women drug takers may become pregnant. Should they do so, they may have to cope with strong social disapproval.

Contraception should not be the sole responsibility of women, but this is expected and even encouraged in many circles. A woman who is intoxicated may be more likely to be cajoled or pressured into casual sex and to forget to take contraceptive precautions. If she is a heavy barbiturate user, the contraceptive action of the pill may in any case be interfered with. A consequence of drug use may be that the menstrual cycle is interrupted. Some women cease to have periods (amenorrhea) and, incorrectly believing themselves to be infertile, see no necessity for contraception. Amenorrhea is especially distressing for some, who suffer emotional consequences as their sense of self-worth is affected by the belief that they can no longer fulfil their role — as defined by others — as women. Menstruation tends to resume some time after the cessation of heavy or chaotic drug use, to the evident relief of some and the annoyance of others.

Women drug takers may also be especially vulnerable to rape and to involvement in exploitative heterosexual relationships over which they can exert little control. On a more positive note, many have loving and healthy relationships which may produce children, planned or unplanned.

Stereotypes of women drug takers invariably suggest that they are worse, sicker, more deviant, or harder to work with than their male counterparts. Despite much evidence to the contrary (Williams 1985) these negative and judgemental beliefs persist and are further compounded when a woman drug taker is pregnant. 'The pregnancy, a visible and inescapable reminder of the client's femininity, triggers feelings and responses as painful and threatening to the clinician as to the client. These reactions may indeed foster an outlook that these women are "hard to work with"' (Williams 1985).

Drug use during pregnancy can present some risk to the foetus as well as the mother-to-be. Hazards may arise from exposure to both acute and chronic effects. An example of the latter is the so-called 'foetal alcohol syndrome' where regular alcohol use during pregnancy is held to increase the risk of certain abnormalities including low birth weight, dysfunction of the central nervous system and facial characteristics. There is some evidence for a corresponding foetal narcotic syndrome, although 'exposure to opiates does not seem to be associated with great hazard to the developing foetus, although regular exposure to this drug is associated with a small-for-date baby with an increased risk of a number of general disorders' (Strang and Moran 1985).

Apart from the effects of chronic toxicity, the foetus may be subject to overdose, intoxication, or withdrawal according to the mother's pattern of use. There may also be a risk to the foetus if the mother is vulnerable to accidents because of her drug use. Research shows that the incidence of low weight or premature birth and morbidity can be significantly reduced through high quality and constant ante-natal care (Finegan 1978).

Some classes of drug, if they regularly cross the placental barrier, may induce physical dependence in the foetus. This gives rise to considerable moral outrage but, if properly managed, withdrawal need not cause distress to the baby, poses no great risk and the experience should have little, if any, long-term consequences (Strang and Moran 1985). The timing of a (medically supervised) withdrawal is important. If it is undertaken during the early months, a spontaneous abortion may occur, whilst withdrawal in the late stages of pregnancy could result in premature labour. A thorough medical assessment and case history may indicate withdrawal during the second trimester or at some point following the birth of the child. Guilt — or delight — on discovering that they are pregnant leads some women to want to stop using straight away. They should be advised against this if they are dependent or use in heavy bouts and be referred for qualified medical advice.

Both workers and relatives also often assume that pregnant women should become drug-free immediately, so demonstrating commitment to parenthood and improving their ability to function effectively. However, users are often at their most vulnerable following detoxification, may not have had time to develop other mechanisms for coping with stress and will anyway be facing an additional range of anxieties because of impending parenthood.

Another potential problem is that infections can be passed from the pregnant mother to the foetus. In particular, the HIV virus responsible for AIDS can be transmitted in this manner. If the mother has shared needles and syringes or had unprotected sexual intercourse with HIV carriers she will be in a high-risk category. In addition, if she is infected, pregnancy will increase the risk of her developing AIDS itself. There is a high possibility that the child will be born infected.

Concern about possible risks to the unborn child should not lead workers into hasty moral judgements and poor practice. More research is needed so that realistic harm minimization responses can be developed. Much of the apposite intervention lies in the domain of medical professionals, and social workers, while familiarizing themselves with the facts and issues should ensure that clients are referred for medical care and advice.

Nevertheless, social workers have a positive role to play. Pregnancy and the months after birth are stressful times, both physically and psychologically. For drug takers, difficulties may be compounded as a result of social stigmatization, guilt, ambivalence towards drug use, the child and perhaps the father. The woman may need considerable support during her pregnancy and post partum when she may be at risk of returning to drug use or of supplementing her agreed dosage to deal with isolation, her sense of inadequacy, disapproval from others and the stress that any woman can experience in nurturing a young baby, perhaps as a single parent and probably with slim financial resources.

She may also need encouragement to initiate and sustain contact with ante- and post-natal care. Health services may not always take a sympathetic view of her situation. It has been observed by many specialist workers that pregnant users often do not come forward immediately for fear of statutory intervention and are frequently reluctant to continue seeing their doctors because of the initial reactions of disapproval they experience. 'You should be put up against a wall and shot' was one general practitioner's response to a sixteen-year-old drug taker.

It is essential that there is adequate liaison and communication between the agencies involved and with the client.

A tragic irony for drug-using parents is that if they seek help because they are concerned that their drug use may be detrimental to their children, then those children may be taken into care, and their parents lose any reason for stabilizing or terminating their drug use. It would be irresponsible to suggest that a parent's heavy and chaotic drug use might not affect parenting, but just as irresponsible to assume that drug takers are intrinsically incapable of caring for their children. Both drug use and children at risk are emotive issues. A combination of the two can present an ethical minefield to workers as they attempt to juggle the needs of everyone involved.

As drug use becomes more widespread, the incidence of referrals to social services involving drug-using parents will increase. Unfortunately, some social service departments automatically place the children of problem drug takers on the at-risk register. This practice has been reinforced by the decision of a Berkshire Magistrates Court in 1985 where it was ruled that a child's development *in utero* was being impaired or neglected because the mother was an addict. The child was made the subject of a care order and the judgement was subsequently upheld by the House of Lords. This decision has important moral, legal and practice implications. The blanket policies which it has encouraged serve to reinforce unhelpful myths and stereotypes, hamper clear assessment and fail to take into account the specific needs and circumstances of any given child or family. An undue focus upon parental drug use which excludes consideration of other factors can mask the existence of parenting skills and resources and also divert attention from other areas which might warrant concern.

Case example: Shirley and Mike

Shirley and Mike had two children, aged 11 years and 18 months respectively. Social services became involved because their health visitor was concerned that the children might have access to drugs, or be at risk when their parents were intoxicated. The workers failed to consider the way in which the older child undertook considerable adult responsibility for the family and that the baby was understimulated and in 'a world of her own'. These points were noted by a specialist non-statutory agency who then found themselves in a very difficult position. They did not wish to support the instigation of care proceedings on the basis of the parents' drug use and assessed that separating the children from their parents would be counter-productive. However, they did want to secure increased support for the parents generally, improving their parenting skills and ensuring that the children's personal development was not further impaired.

*

Children may start to look after their parents at an early age, possibly truanting or sacrificing friendships and normal childhood activities to do so. They may collect prescriptions from the pharmacist, deal with overdoses and look after younger siblings. Despite the stress this can cause, they may feel it disloyal to confide in others, although it is not unknown for children to approach agencies for help with their drug-taking parents.

An article in *Community Care* (Dubble, Dun, Aldridge and Kearney 1987) drew attention to a similar issue and noted that children who are regularly present when drug dealing takes place in their home environment are often able to form superficial relationships with adults, but have difficulty in forming deeper ones with anybody. The authors suggest that one indicator of concern can be very young children's development of elaborate fantasy worlds to compensate for their limited contact with peers or non-drug-taking adults.

Spurred on by the growing concern about childcare issues, social workers from drug dependence units in the south-east of England have suggested guidelines for assessment in cases involving the children of drug-using parents. They state that 'in families where likely parental drug use is seen as a major factor of concern, a comprehensive assessment of the relationship between the pattern of drug use and the level of child care is needed' and that 'in cases where drug use is seen as a significant factor, SSDs should be encouraged to liaise or consult with a specialist drug worker' (Dubble *et al* 1987). They also stress that, in their experience, parental drug use does not automatically indicate child neglect or abuse and that 'some drug using parents are good parents in all the usual senses.'

In an article introducing the guidelines (SCODA 1986), Rosemary Morle suggests that they may be given to and discussed with clients, so that they are fully aware of the expectations placed upon them. The preface to the guidelines strongly states that drug use does not automatically indicate child neglect or abuse, and argues against automatically initiating the child abuse procedure and registering the children, as this will deter parents from seeking help. The guidelines allow for a comprehensive assessment of the relationship between parental drug use and child care, and can be applied according to the circumstances of each family. The assessment should include:

1. *The pattern of parental drug use:*
    Is there a drug-free parent or supportive partner?
    Type, quantity and method of administration of drugs.
    Whether drug use is relatively 'stable' or 'chaotic' - i.e. swings between states of severe intoxication and periods of withdrawal and/ or poly-drug use, including alcohol.
    Are the levels of care different from when the parent is a non-user

2. *Accommodation and home environment:*
    Is the accommodation adequate for children?
    Are parents ensuring that rent and bills are paid?
    Does the family remain in one locality or move frequently and why?
    Are other drug users sharing the accommodation?
    Is the family living in a drug-using community?

3. *Provision of basic necessities:*
    Is there adequate food, clothing, and warmth for the children?
    Are the children attending school regularly?
    Are the children's emotional needs being adequately met?
    Are the children assuming parental responsibility?

4. *How the drugs are procured:*
    Are the children being left alone whilst the parents are procuring drugs?
    Are the children being taken to places where they can be deemed to be at risk?
    How much are the drugs costing and how is the money obtained?
    Are the premises being used for selling drugs, prostitution etc.?
    Are the parents allowing their premises to be used by other drug users?

5. *Health risks:*
    Where are the drugs normally kept?
    Are the parents injecting drugs?
    Are the syringes shared? How are they disposed of?

Are the parents aware of the health risks attached to injecting or otherwise using drugs?

6. *Family's social network and support systems*
Do parents and children associate primarily with other drug users, non-drug users or both?
Are relatives aware of the drug use? Are they supportive?
Will parents accept help from the relatives and other professional/ voluntary agencies involved?

7. *When intervention is necessary:*
Automatic intervention deters contact.
Are there grounds under one's own local authority's care procedures?
Are these appropriate for assessment?

8. *The parents' perceptions of the situation:*
Do they see their drug use as harmful to themselves or their children?
Do parents place their own needs before those of their children?

Clearly paragraph seven of the guidelines refers to formal care proceedings and the Non-accidental Injuries register. There may be areas where other forms of intervention could be appropriate. For example, assisting with practical difficulties over accommodation or finances, nursery places, health education, or onward referral. There may well be an assumption, on the part of both social worker and parents, that if the parents are detoxified they will be better able to look after their children. This is not always so, at least in the short term, if, although physically detoxified, they remain psychologically dependent and vulnerable.

11 Developing Responses with the Client

Clients may not recognize that a problem exists, or while knowing that all is not well, may yet be unable to identify the cause of their distress with any degree of specificity. The more chaotic, or simply muddled, the client is, the greater the need for the worker's approach to be structured. Properly used, structure allows for flexibility and security for both client and worker, enabling them to develop a greater understanding of the situation, identify where problems might lie and look for ways forward. This chapter discusses some models or frameworks, which embody the basic orientation that drug use need not necessarily or automatically be problematic, that individuals differ widely in their patterns of use, that a variety of problems can emerge whose presence or absence in any particular case needs to be investigated rather than assumed, and that although abstinence may be the preferred goal in some cases, it is not the only possible one. In any given case, harm minimization, and the maximization of stability and control, may be more realistic and appropriate aims.

The problem drug taker
The model of the 'problem drug taker', defined in Chapter 3, provides a useful tool for social workers. It avoids value-laden terms like 'addict' or 'sick', places drug-taking in a wider context than the purely medical, and breaks down the phrase 'drug problem' into its component parts, which often turn out to be the kinds of problem with which social workers are equipped to deal. It also allows room for the possibility that an individual's drug use may not be problematic at all.

Thus, worker and client can:

1. Examine whether drug use masks, worsens, or stems from problem areas that existed prior to drug use (for example, social relationships, employment difficulties, emotional problems);

2. Examine whether problems - legal, social, psychological or physical - arise from drug use;

3. Examine which facet of use (intoxication, regular excessive use, or dependence) is associated with problems;

4.   Clarify where change is needed to minimize harm, promote stability, or allow more constructive methods of coping;

5.   Clarify which agency is best suited to respond to the types of problem present.

The focus will depend on the individual. There are times when drug use is associated with pre-existing and deep-rooted problems, but this is by no means always the case. Neither is it always appropriate to investigate this possibility if the client's more immediate problems are overwhelming, or when it seems advantageous to look forward rather than back.

Self-monitoring of excessive consumption, intoxication and dependence
Many users have only a hazy idea of their pattern of consumption, of the factors that precipitate problematic drug-taking for them, and of the connection between use and any resultant difficulties they encounter. Asking them to self-monitor their use can be very useful in identifying areas which need attention. It has the further advantage that, having taken an active part in the process, clients are likely to have a greater investment in the conclusions drawn from the exercise than would be the case if they were merely the passive recipients of workers' interpretations.

One way of doing this is for the client to keep a diary. This can be a valuable tool in establishing current patterns of use, possible areas of concern and potential responses to them. It enables clients to clarify the nature and extent of their drug use by asking themselves the following questions about their use over the previous day, week, or longer period:

What did I use?
How much did I use/How much did it cost?
When did I use, at what points and times of the day?
Why did I use?
What did I want to feel?
How did I feel before I used?
How did I feel afterwards - better, the same, worse?
Were there any long-term consequences?
What could I have done instead of using?
What would have encouraged me not to use?
How could I have avoided the situation?

The task can be modified to suit particular circumstances and can be made as complex or simple as the situation dictates. Clients who have poor literacy skills might feel intimidated at the prospect of keeping detailed records, and others feel overwhelmed by the task even at its most basic level. Therefore it might be appropriate to remove some of the areas, to simply encourage the client to think about them, or for worker and client to address them together in sessions. On the other hand, some clients derive a great deal of satisfaction or sense of achievement from keeping a diary. It allows them a greater sense of control in confronting the real issues and, on a more mundane level, it is at the very least a useful time-filler. Whichever form clients choose to employ, they and the worker should analyze the information together. Clients may reach a closer understanding of the circumstances that lead to use and to any immediate or long-term negative consequences; and, if they wish to exercise control, discover methods of doing so. Over time a comparison of weekly accounts may show how the client is making progress, for example by cutting out one dose in the day, or by finding an alternative way of coping with a situation.

This technique will also highlight that the cues and pressures which motivate the client towards excessive drug use, stability, or abstinence may vary daily. It is useful to discuss this, drawing up a list of the pros and cons of drug use and asking clients to list and prioritize those things that influence them to increase or decrease their drug use. From this can emerge ideas about the areas that need to be changed or reinforced. Clients' ability to identify the pressures and situations which are likely to precipitate problem drug use is particularly important if abstinence or moderation are to be sustained (Marlatt and George 1984).

Experimental, recreational and dependent drug use
It is vital to remember that drug takers vary widely in their choice of drugs, the circumstances and frequency with which they use, the reasons for their use and the type and severity of problems that they experience as a consequence.

One model that is helpful in establishing this is to view drug-taking as encompassing a spectrum of behaviours which can be categorized into experimental, recreational or compulsive dependent forms of use. A number of variations exist on this theme and are to be found throughout the literature on understanding and responding to problem drinkers and drug takers (e.g. Jaffe 1977, Pearson *et al.* 1987).

By definition, anyone's initial use of a drug is experimental. For reasons of fashion, availability, peer group pressure, rebellion, or simple curiosity, the decision is made, often casually, to sample a new experience. The choice of drug or drugs may be relatively random, the experimenter's knowledge of the drug's effects, required dosage and possible dangers may be imperfect and the user will not know at first whether the experience will be enjoyable or not. If it is not enjoyable, use will be discontinued unless the person is prepared to persevere in the expectation that a taste for the experience will develop in time, or unless external factors, such as the desire to be accepted by peers or acquire a particular image, outweigh the unpleasant or uninteresting drug effects (consider here the early experiences that many readers will have had with alcohol or tobacco). By its very nature, experimental use is a short-lived phase. Many, perhaps the majority of people who have ever used an 'illegal' drug, drop out at this point and confine their future consumption to the more socially acceptable, though not less dangerous, drugs – alcohol and tobacco. Some, however, having decided that the drug is to their taste, will move on to become recreational drug users.

Recreational drug use is both more specific and more controlled than the preceding stage. The individual will have discovered a preference for a particular drug, learnt how to administer it and appreciate its effects and have at least some knowledge of its dangers and how to avoid them. The drug will tend to be used at certain times and places (at weekends, at parties, during visits to a disco or concert), as a pleasureable adjunct to the user's social life. Generally, the user will not experience any serious adverse medical or social consequences due directly to the drug, although legal and social reaction may, of course present difficulties. Drug use is but one aspect of the user's life, one activity among many, and one seen as unproblematic, enjoyable and no proper concern of anybody else. Again, a comparison with the way in which most people in our society use alcohol is pertinent.

A percentage of those who have reached the stage of recreational use will discover that the drug can function as a means of helping them to cope with or avoid problems, both psychological and external. At this point, there is a risk of them moving on into dependent/compulsive use. To some extent, most of us use drugs in this way from time to time– the stiff drink, the 'nice cup of tea', the occasional tranquillizer to help us manage a difficult situation – but for the dependent drug taker, resort to drugs becomes the almost automatic response to any distress. Life now begins to centre around the drug, and other concerns and interests become increasingly peripheral. Use becomes less controlled, the user may become less discriminating about which drug is used, and a pattern of multi-drug use may develop. Psychological and perhaps physical dependence will be present. As the user becomes more and more reliant upon the comforting familiarity of the drug experience, the problems for which drug use was seen as a solution will be exacerbated and new problems caused directly by drug use will emerge. Social and financial matters will suffer and the user is likely to become isolated from all but the company of other users. Although perhaps well aware of the role that drug use plays in the downward spiral, there is often great resistance on the part of dependent users to any suggestion that they should stop taking drugs, since to do so would, as they see it, leave them with overwhelming problems while removing the one reliable source of comfort available to them. For others the attraction of the drug, of the state of intoxication and the associated life-style, remains uppermost.

Between recreational and dependent/compulsive use, there is an undefined area where users are slipping from one to the other and back again. Over time, many drug dependents regain relative control over their use as the pressures they experience alter or their ability to cope with them improves. Conversely, recreational users may drift unwittingly into a pattern of compulsive use. The careers of many users exhibit a pattern of alternation between dependence, abstinence and recreational use.

Where any given client is located on this continuum is of great importance in assessment, as it will provide pointers to the kinds of problem likely to be present and to appropriate ways of handling them. The rest of this chapter examines possible social work responses to experimental, recreational and dependent/compulsive drug takers. It should be noted that although particular types of problem are associated with each stage of drug use, individuals can experience a good many of them at any stage, so that while the use of health education and harm reduction approaches, for instance, are discussed in the context of experimental and recreational use, they may also find application in working with dependent and chaotic users.

Experimental and recreational use

Experimentation and challenge to adult value systems are very much part of growing up, integral to the maturation process that at times inevitably exposes experimenters to risks from which the adult world would rather shelter them. Doubtless some form of experimental use of psychoactive substances has always been incorporated into this process by many young people. As the use of one substance becomes more acceptable to society, so another, often apparently more harmful, takes its place. In the past, countless teenagers have made themselves bilious on cigarettes behind the bike shed, doggedly downed quantities of cooking sherry or, more recently, smoked cannabis. In the 1980s concern has focused upon the experimental use of solvents and heroin. Research shows that most people confine their drug use to this stage and few go on to develop long-term problems (Jaffe 1977). But public attitudes are such that responses to experimental use based on a rational assessment of the probable outcome and risks are likely to encounter considerable opposition.

Case example: John, aged 15

John's parents were panic-stricken to discover that their only son was sniffing glue with friends. After an angry and tearful scene, they immediately alerted the school, social services and the family doctor, and treatment plans were hastily considered. In fact John stopped sniffing of his own accord, finding the experience unrewarding, and soon afterwards made the transition to an acceptable form of adult intoxication - alcohol. Everyone breathed a sigh of relief, treatment plans were dropped and his father actively encouraged this sign of 'normality'. He was drinking five or six pints a night.

*

Here, over-reaction when solvents were involved was replaced by corresponding under-reaction when they were superseded by alcohol. Apart from specific health risks, if there had been underlying problems then they would not have gone away simply because the substance had changed. The fact that John's alcohol use was encouraged neglected the fact that his consumption was both illegal and at a risk level. By not following up on this, an important health education and harm reduction role was ignored. In addition, investigation of whether John's intemperate drinking pattern was an expression of adolescent experimentation and bravado, or whether more serious problems underlay it, might have been called for.

Experimental users are usually referred for help by others who are concerned about their activities. This is also true for recreational users. In control of their drug use, involved in other activities and relationships more central to their lives – their families, friends, work – they will usually see no need to seek help. If their activities come to light at all, it will usually be as the result of action by a friend or relative, by a professional who has unearthed evidence of drug use in the course of other investigations, or through involvement with the legal system. These users may be either puzzled or resentful that what they believe to be a harmless activity should become the occasion for social work intervention; in many cases these feelings will be justified.

Nevertheless, although experimental or recreational drug takers are not dependent on drugs, they may be facing some actual or potential problems. Even if this is not the case, the fact that they have been referred at all implies that there is a problem for *someone,* and workers should consider whether they need to respond. If they do, then it will probably be more fruitful to focus on harm reduction and changes in the environment, than on pathology or personal change.

Harm minimization
Experimental users, because of their ignorance and lack of experience, may be at some physical risk of overdose or accident. This may occur because they are unclear about safe dosages and means of administration; because they are unprepared to deal with the drug's effects; or because they are taking the drug in places where it is unsafe to be intoxicated, such as a canal or railway embankment, the central heating vent of a high-rise flat (to keep their activity secret), on the walkways of housing estates or traffic-laden streets (because they want to be seen, or be intimidating). Similar problems can arise for dependent users who have lost control. The hazards associated with unsafe injection methods are also pertinent here, particularly as they concern AIDS. Clear information about how to reduce or avoid hazards while continuing to use can be appropriate. 'Teaching About a Volatile Situation' (ISDD 1981) suggests how this might be done in the case of solvent use. This approach has been criticised as condoning and colluding with drug use, but

this is not a helpful or accurate interpretation. Users are unlikely to stop simply because they are told to and may continue using in a potentially life-threatening way. It is surely preferable to improve the probability of their staying alive and relatively unharmed until they can make a decision to cease their substance use, and to ensure that their decisions are made from an informed basis.

Secondary prevention
The worker should also assess the likelihood of experimental and recreational users spiralling down into more problematic dependent/compulsive patterns of use. Are they worried about anything? Are there difficulties at home, school, work, or in a relationship? Are they feeling insecure, unhappy, depressed? Is their development impaired in any way? Are they unemployed or truanting? How do they fill their time? Have they ever taken drugs to deal with any of these issues or are they likely to? Do they always use alone, do they attach undue importance to the drug or the ritual surrounding its use? Is the pattern of use and type of drug such that they will become physically dependent? For example, do they use heroin every day, or is consumption likely to increase from intermittent use at parties or the weekend, to several times a week? If the answer to any of these questions is yes, the implications should be discussed with the client and, in addition to harm reduction and decision-making approaches, time should be given to making any needed changes in the environment and the way that the client responds to it, and to developing coping mechanisms and personal resources.

Decision-making and alternative activities
Most people are offered drugs for the first time by friends or acquaintances (Hartnoll and Gray 1986; Caplin and Woodward 1986). In such circumstances it can be very difficult to 'just say no'. To do so can leave a young person isolated as the only one in the group not taking drugs. It may therefore be appropriate to help clients to improve their decision-making skills so that they have both accurate information and the personal self-esteem to enable them to refuse drugs, should they wish to. Both the Institute for the Study of Drug Dependence (ISDD 1982) and the Teachers Advisory Council on Alcohol and Drug Education (TACADE 1984) have produced educational material designed to increase decision-making skills.

Many people take drugs for fun and excitement or because they are bored. This is an important consideration when unemployment levels are so high. Drugs are an excellent time-filler, and where more conventional paths are unavailable the role of drug user can provide an alternative career with its own excitements and pay-offs (Preble and Casey 1969). What can the worker offer in place of drugs and the associated life-style? The answer is often little enough, but despite the paucity of resources for the unemployed and young people in many areas of the country it is useful to identify alternative activities that may appeal to the individual or group of recreational users, to encourage their participation and suggest, or if necessary make, relevant contacts. A youth and community work approach is more appropriate here than traditional social work intervention.

Effect on others/management problems
Faced with a drug-related problem, the worker should always ask who it is a problem for. Drug use frequently manifests itself as a problem, not for the user, but for significant others in the immediate environment. In turn, their reactions may create problems for the hitherto trouble-free user. Families, partners and friends are affected by experimental and recreational use and may seek help, incorrectly believing the drug taker to be addicted. They should be encouraged to share their anxieties and to explain why they are worried, and appropriate reassurance and information should be given. They may also benefit from contact with others who have had similar experiences, though this may be more relevant to the families of dependent users. It might become apparent that the drug, or the user, is being made a scapegoat, or that there are significant underlying problems in the relationship (to which the drug use may be contributing), in which case counselling or family therapy might be indicated.

Experimental or recreational users may also find themselves pathologized by professional carers, when the real problem is to be found in the staff's inability to handle drug use within the agency, their attitude to drugs and drug takers, the lack of an agency policy, or the presence of a positively unhelpful one. This is a situation which occurs frequently in residential hostels of all types. One has also heard youth workers boasting that there are 'no glue sniffers or drug takers in my club' and then discovered that this is because all such miscreants are refused entry. Such a policy, although understandable as an attempt to protect non-drug-using members, renders it impossible to do any work with, and further isolates, a group who may be at some risk of coming to harm. Where individual staff members within a team have radically differing attitudes and responses to instances of drug use, the team can be split and service delivery suffer. All such instances are best dealt with by training and the formulation and implementation of appropriate policy which balances the needs of the drug users against those of the agency and other attenders or residents.

Compulsive/dependent use
Although most people who get that far either continue as recreational users, or simply slip out of drug use altogether, for some the purpose of drug use shifts from being a source of pleasure or an aid to social discourse, to being primarily a solution to problems, or the sole focus of their lives. If identified in time, this process can often be interrupted, but some people become totally enmeshed in drug use and in a complex web of difficulties from which, as

far as they and often their social workers can see, there is no apparent escape. The drug taker appears no longer in a position to exert much control or real choice. Yates (1982) suggests that the essential difference between recreational and compulsive use 'is typified by the difference between the search for excitement and challenge as a complement to one's life and the retreat from the threat and uncertainty of day-to-day existence into a comfortingly predictable sensation through ritual and physical intoxication.'

A complex relationship

That drug-dependent users should be ambivalent about stopping is scarcely surprising. They may perhaps no longer derive much active enjoyment from their drugs (although, contrary to puritan myth, many still do), they may even recognize that their problems stem from or are exacerbated by their use. But the status quo still appears preferable to an unpredictable world without the drug which has come to be a solution to real and imagined distress. Their self-esteem and physical state may be so low that they simply cannot summon up the energy to make changes. The relationship between user and drug is complex and may mask personal and social problems that they have little desire to face up to or confidence in their ability to overcome. An analogy can be drawn with the situation of a couple enmeshed in an unhappy and destructive relationship. Although one partner or the other may be desperate to end it, it may offer sufficient compensations, and the prospect of what life would be like afterwards may be so frightening, to ensure that the decision to part is endlessly postponed. It can be many years before such a liaison is finally dissolved, its end precipitated perhaps by internal factors, perhaps by the removal or creation of external sources of support. The timing and circumstances of the break – whether sooner or later – will differ from relationship to relationship and the same is true of the relationships between addicts and their drug. This should not be taken to imply that drug takers have to reach rock bottom before they can change their life-style.

Some may have a love/hate relationship with their drug and yet experience a deep sense of loss if they cease to take it. The drug was the only predictable and certain element in their life. Workers have employed a form of bereavement counselling to allow the client to work through their grief, anger, and fears for the future. Other users have been reluctant to leave the relative safety of their addict identity and life-style for the hard and distressing path that leads to change, with no certainty that their quality of life will be improved. Some will be unwilling to move from a passive role of victim and addict and assume responsibility for themselves.

The complexity of the relationship is usefully illustrated by two cycles, or positive feedback loops, the Addiction and the Self-Regard Cycles which operate both to sustain dependent drug use and to intensify the problems which result from it (Peele 1981). See Figures 11.1 and 11.2.

Faced with a problem, the dependent user's habitual response is to take a drug. While intoxicated, awareness of or concern about the problem is blotted out. In effect, the problem is temporarily solved or shelved. Because the user is intoxicated, the ability to respond to the problem on a practical level is decreased, the problem worsened, and additional problems may ensue. The cycle then repeats.

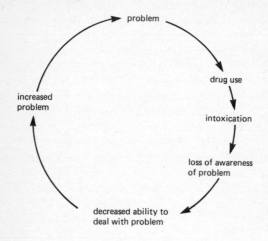

Figure 11.1 The addiction cycle:

At the same time that the above cycle is operating, a similar process takes place on the psychological level.

Figure 11.2 Self-regard cycle:

Many drug-dependent individuals suffer from poor self-esteem, worsened by their apparent inability to escape from uncontrolled drug use and change their situation through their own efforts. Drug use allows a temporary alleviation of these feelings, at the expense of confirming and worsening them once the effects have worn off. The increased feelings of guilt and self-denigration then precipitate further use.

The worker must work with the client to try to break both these cycles, looking for ways in which self-esteem can be improved, identifying situations which are particularly threatening or destructive, and helping the client develop other ways of dealing with emotional and practical problems.

For many dependent users, poor self-esteem can be crippling — they do not aim for change because they are certain that they will fail, believe that success occurs by accident and not through their own actions, or that they do not deserve success and the rewards that will ensue. The worker should help to improve opportunities for good experiences, drawing upon assessment information about periods of unimpaired functioning, happiness, achievement, and interests; reinforce changes and progress, however minimal they may appear to others, and assist clients to deal with positive learning experiences which might at first appear alien and threatening.

Clearly responses to this type of drug use will necessarily be different from the preceding categories, and a number of factors should be taken into account.

'Hopeless cases': the need for good supervision

Often when faced with a client who is a compulsive dependent drug taker, the worker is completely at a loss, not knowing where to begin, or how to start making sense out of the muddle. Often clients are not really sure exactly what is wrong. When asked why they take drugs, the answer is likely to be some variation on the theme of 'for fun' or 'I don't know', or 'because I'm hooked'. They appear unmotivated, or are apathetic or unrealistic about how to make changes. All this translates into a mutual sense of powerlessness infecting both worker and client and the notion of 'hopeless case' ensues. This must be avoided, for worker expectation can influence clients' self-esteem, reinforcing the belief that they are only good at failing. Thorley (1983) highlights this theme:

> The idea of 'hopeless cases' can ... provide a slippery slope towards client exclusion and nihilism. Clients adopt workers' nihilism just as they take up workers' enthusiasm and hope. A successful client career in rehabilitation is like a successful career in medicine or social work: it needs to be managed with care and concern for the individual, and with not a little enthusiasm.

Workers can sometimes feel isolated and overwhelmed, even exasperated, in their work with drug takers and their families. Access to good supervision is then vital. Workers may need to explore their own attitudes and frustration;

their reactions to apparent manipulation - which may in fact be a conflict of views, or testing out; their feelings of responsibility for a client; whether they are being overly empathetic and taking the principles of non-conditional positive regard too far; or whether they are simply at a loss as to how to proceed. Workers should also use supervision to reappraise their expectations and notion of success. Perhaps because drug use is such an emotive issue, many workers feel that they should aspire to a 100% success rate as measured by a sustained drug-free state for their clients. This is unrealistic and places an unfair burden on both worker and client. How many have comparable expectations for other less 'dramatic' client groups?

Motivation: The relationship between client, worker, drug and situation
To avoid such pitfalls, workers may need to reappraise their expectations and understanding of the term 'motivation'. With this client group, perhaps more than with any other, it is absolutely necessary that the client is involved and has as much control as possible in the process. To do something *to* the client is less likely to succeed than working together towards negotiated and agreed ends. If clients believe that a desirable change has been achieved by their own efforts, the prospect of continued progress is greatly increased. The sense of self-efficacy seems to be the crucial factor in maintaining successful change (Bandura 1977). In work with apparently apathetic, demoralized, or ambivalent clients, the need for a structured approach is paramount and the model of the 'problem drug taker', discussed earlier in this chapter, is helpful in this regard. If a problem can be broken down into its component parts, then it is immediately more accessible and less threatening to the worker and, more crucially, to the client.

Clients often apparently lack any motivation to change, or exhibit a large degree of ambivalence. This can be frustrating for the worker but should not be taken as proof that the client does not want or deserve help, or that they are not in need of it. Motivation is best thought of, not as some mysterious attribute which the client either does or does not possess, but as the outcome of complex and changing interactions between the client's self-image, the drug, the relationship of client and worker, and the client's current life situation. A number of points should be considered in understanding and harnessing motivation.

1. Who says that there is a problem and that changes are necessary? Clients may not have a problem, or may refuse to admit to one because of the way it has come to light. They may seek help because someone else wants them to. They may genuinely believe that they do not have a problem, or that their problems are unconnected with drug use, or be afraid to admit it to themselves or others, as to do so would leave them vulnerable and facing painful decisions.

Here, the worker can show acceptance, initiate a dialogue around different perceptions of the situation and the client's fantasies of how they are seen, and adopt a preventative and educational role. It is common for drug takers to become more willing to confront their drug use, or ask about treatment and rehabilitation options, if they have had the opportunity to 'test out' their first point of contact and to focus on their immediate practical concerns. The client must want to make changes and the worker's role may be to help the client to recognize any problems arising from drug use and suggest how the client's quality of life may be improved. This should be done tactfully and not in a way that will strip the client of current survival skills without access to alternatives. There may come a time when the worker feels that a more confrontative approach is needed to encourage the client to adopt a more realistic attitude. Workers should beware, though, of enforcing their own perspectives and value systems. They should also recall that motivation is a dynamic process and that commitment to change may increase or diminish according to many variables.

What are you offering? In suggesting that help will be offered, practical or otherwise, the worker should not promise or imply that magic answers are available, thus setting up false hopes. Drug takers are accustomed to immediate gratification and may be put off by waiting lists for detoxification or rehabilitation programmes, let alone by the length of time they may have to spend in them, or the many steps involved in achieving and sustaining drug-freeness. Workers may inadvertently obfuscate this issue through their own expectations and frustration at the apparent lack of progress. Whilst some clients may be in a position to make changes relatively swiftly and without continued support, others may want and/or need this for many months or years, even after they have become drug-free.

Goal-setting and work styles should be aimed towards meeting the client's needs, not those of the worker or agency. Workers should be prepared to be eclectic, using non-directive or directive counselling, social skills or problem-solving techniques, groupwork, family therapy, crisis intervention or harm reduction methods, practical assistance and so on, as appropriate, and be ready to accept that another agency may be better fitted to respond to part or all of the problem. The inflexible application of favourite or familiar techniques to each and every case easily leads to the situation where all successes are credited to the virtues of the worker or programme and all failures laid at the door of the client's lack of 'motivation' (Miller 1983)

Workers should — for clients certainly will — ask themselves what is being offered in place of drugs? What is so good about being drug-free? For people who do not experience problems with their drug use and for those whom drug-freeness would leave desolate and overwhelmed with misery, abstinence is not an attractive proposition. What else will provide fun, excitement, friends, an identity, a sense of belonging, and fill up their time? What else will mask problems, take away personal responsibility, make life bearable? If the drug is taken away and nothing else changes, what is the point of staying drug-free? Users need to believe that the drug-free life on offer will provide at least minimally greater rewards than would continued use if they are to be able to make a rational commitment to abstinence.

3. Life-style Drug takers' life-styles can significantly influence the types of problem that they encounter and the prognosis for achieving change. For example, if someone has stable accommodation, employment and supportive drug-free partners (and many do), their chances of detoxifying satisfactorily at home without professional back-up are relatively high. However, if they live with other addicts in a squat with no physical comforts or support, then they will probably find it more difficult, even if they possess a high degree of 'motivation' (Blenheim Project 1982). The remarks in Chapter 3 about the degree to which the severity of withdrawal symptoms are influenced by psychological and situational factors are relevant here. Drug users should not be expected to behave more heroically than the rest of of humankind; sometimes the pressures militating against success are just too great to withstand. A good number of users find it difficult or impossible to withdraw in the community, despite determined efforts. In such cases, efforts should be made to secure in-patient detoxification, or at least to provide as much support as possible during and after withdrawal.

If clients' lives revolve around drug use, then they will prioritize associated tasks (procuring the drug and obtaining the money to buy it, finding needles, arranging deals and avoiding the police) above attending interviews with their social worker or drug dependence unit. This does not necessarily indicate a lack of desire for change, merely a rational ordering (from the user's point of view) of conflicting commitments. This can be especially distressing for users' families, who have often gone to great lengths to persuade them to seek help, and feel rejected and disillusioned by such behaviour. In these circumstances it is difficult to make any form of intervention sound sufficiently attractive, and even if the client has some commitment, this may easily wane because of other pressures.

It is difficult to sustain a decision to control or abstain from use if all one's contacts still take drugs. The individual is a threat to the group who fear change in any form, possible exposure, or the need to confront their own problems. It is common for peers to place implicit or explicit pressure on someone to continue using or to return to the fold. This is a typical group response — witness the abstainer falling to the pressure of drinking acquaintances in the pub. Neither is it easy for people with a history of drug dependence to strike up new relationships. They have lost sight of the necessary social skills and self-esteem, they cannot discuss long periods of their lives for fear of rejection. They have not got other interests or the money to develop them. It is far from easy to make new friends to order, and they can become very isolated. All these factors increase the likelihood of relapse.

Strategies to help the client to maintain abstinence or moderation should emphasize the development of coping skills and self-esteem, the ability to recognize high-risk situations for relapse, environmental changes (e.g. new accommodation, a new social circle), and new interests and involvements in work, education, job training, hobbies, sports, etc. Lapses back into use should be treated as learning opportunities, rather than indications of total failure. Where a client is consistently unsuccessful in sustaining control over drug use, referral to residential rehabilitation should be considered.

4. Goal setting Clients may take an impulsive decision to stop taking drugs, or workers may suggest this objective, without any real assessment of whether this is the best course of action at that moment. Clients may not realise that there can be many steps from chaotic use to sustained and trouble-free abstinence. Or they may be so overwhelmed by their situation that they are unable to envisage any solution. If the worker is over-optimistic in proposing goals, the client will inadvertently be set up to fail. The client's interest may then wane as the possibility of attaining the unrealistic goal recedes and the inappropriateness of the helping strategy becomes clear.

The preparation and negotiation of goals is as important as the goals themselves. The process may take place over several sessions and will be subject to review. The following points should be considered:

(i)   Client and worker should discuss how each perceives the situation, the problem, the drug use, and connections between them.

(ii) They should reach some agreement on how they view the situation and how much significance should be afforded to different factors.

(iii) Problem areas should be broken down and prioritized; goals should be set for each problem area, or area for change, and these too should be prioritized.

(iv) Are the goals realistic? Do they arise from the client's needs? Realistic goals allow the clients to achieve success and will encourage them to continue with a confusing and painful process, where progress can seem very slow, or even negligible. The client should be encouraged to take a positive view of any achievement – for example, dealing with a situation without recourse to drugs, or cutting out a customary dose. One should also be aware that the outcome of decision-making and goal-setting will be influenced by the mood of the client at the time that these are agreed. For example, if clients are very depressed or very excited, they may be unduly pessimistic or optimistic about what they can or should aim for. The worker should try to create a sense of safety and equilibrium from which realistic objectives can be formed.

(v)   Does the client accept the validity of making agreed changes, and understand the processes involved?

(vi) What does the client believe are the advantages and disadvantages of making changes – particularly if they involve modifying or ceasing drug use?

(vii)   Does the client have the personal strength, self-esteem, resources and support networks to achieve change?

(viii) Goals can and should be reviewed from time to time – for example, initially a client may accept the validity of modifying injecting and sexual practices because of the risk of contracting the HIV virus. Later, he may be inclined to clarify a new set of goals, such as giving some shape to the day, taking more care of health and appearance, reducing consumption, attending literacy classes, etc.

(ix)   Abstinence may be the preferred goal for some users and workers. But it may not be appropriate for everyone at the time they seek help. They should not be viewed as failures because they do not seek or sustain a drug-free lifestyle. Their wish to reach this state and their ability to attain it may develop in time.

(x)   Many of the above points can go towards establishing a contract of agreed aims, objectives, and areas of responsibility.

Drug, person and environment
The above discussion of motivation suggests the many factors that need to be taken into account when trying to understand and modify an individual's drug use. They can be categorized under three headings: the drug, the person and the environment. Understanding their relationship, relative importance and potential for causing, sustaining, or resolving problems can be the key to successful intervention.

The drug
Are users at risk because of patterns of use, toxic effects, impaired functioning? Are they in control of their use? Is the drug the central component of their life-style? What effects do they desire from the drug and are these achieved? What is the attraction of the particular sensation and of the activities associated with drug use? For example, amphetamines may allow shy and inhibited people to feel the life and soul of the party. Do steps need to be taken to stabilize consumption or modify methods of use (for example, needle-sharing) to minimize harm? What other activities or interests (relaxation techniques, assertion training, sports, etc.) might be considered as replacements for some or all of the functions that drug use fulfils?

The person
What are clients' views of themselves and of their place in the world? What are their expectations of life? How can clients' personal resources be maximized so as to allow more control over external problems and internal conflicts? How can they be enabled to make changes in the environment, perhaps by obtaining improved accommodation, by assistance with budgeting, etc.? Help with literacy problems and social skills training may improve

their chances of access to employment, education and community activities. This in turn may improve their self-image and sense of worth. Clients may reach a clearer understanding of their problems and difficulties through counselling or rehabilitation. Are personal and emotional problems being caused, masked or added to drug use? Is their personal growth and development being impaired by their drug use, leaving them deskilled and with a paucity of alternative coping mechanisms?

The environment
What circumstances influence the frequency and intensity of use? The family, housing problems, relationships with partners, unemployment and financial problems, pressure from peers, availability and many other factors may contribute. It is difficult to stop using if outside pressures remain the same, if friends urge to resume use or, in the case of tranquillizer dependence, the family is ambivalent about one's desire to stop. Can changes be made in the environment to reduce the pressures for continuing to use in a problematic way, or to increase the positive features that would buttress stability or abstinence? What resources can be drawn upon — family, friends, helping agencies, adult education and training opportunities? Does the client need to be rehoused, or to move away from the area temporarily or permanently?

Prescribed drugs: minor tranquillizers
This chapter has largely drawn on work with illicit or non-medical users of drugs. Nevertheless the frameworks can be applied where clients wish to take more control over their prescribed drug use with a possible view to living without it. This is perhaps more explicit with regard to people on medication because of their previous unsanctioned use, but it is also true where minor tranquillizers are involved. The relationship between drug, person and environment is equally pertinent. It is, however, helpful to consider some additional points.
1. The majority of tranquillizers are issued to women, and there is growing evidence that black and working-class women are more likely to be prescribed tranquillizers than offered alternatives such as therapy or practical assistance.
2. If a client expresses a wish to come off tranquillizers it is important to clarify the exact nature of the prescription. In fact the drugs involved may be major tranquillizers or antidepressants, rather than benzodiazepines. These are totally different categories of drugs and require different handling. The worker should consult the GP, hospital doctor or psychiatrist concerned. It may be that such medication is the only way that the client can function in the community. There are times when this treatment may be abused, and local mental health groups will be in a position to advise on the appropriate course of action.

3. It should not be forgotten that tranquillizers can have a valid role in the short-term treatment of emotional distress.

4. It is advisable for people to withdraw from tranquillizers gradually, preferably with medical supervision and support. Clients might, however, find their doctors unsympathetic to their plans, and the worker could usefully assist by training clients to become more assertive and possibly by accompanying them to the surgery.

5. Many people are on tranquillizers for many years. Both they and their families may be very ambivalent about attempts to withdraw. They often have to face discouragement from partners or children who are threatened by the 'new' person who emerges after twenty years of sedation.

6. The process of detoxifying and the following drug-free period can be distressing and bewildering, both as a result of the physical withdrawal and because emotions which have been suppressed for so long bubble to the surface. Furthermore, any problems that might have arisen, or which possibly gave rise to medical treatment in the first place – whether it was appropriate or not – will now have to be faced. This can be hard in view of the client's vulnerable state, the fact that many tranquillizer users are afforded and accept a victim identity and have a poor sense of self-worth, and may have little access to support as they change role from carer to being in need of care.

7. Many tranquillizer users reap great benefit from self-help groups where they can share their experiences, while others derive help from one-to-one professional relationships. Relaxation classes and other mechanisms for dealing with stress can be extremely helpful.

8. Tranquillizers can be a bridge to other forms of drug use. For example, young women who are prescribed librium may find that increasing a single dose and combining it with alcohol can result in a pleasureable effect, so awakening an interest in recreational drug use. Others, possibly using their parents' drug use as a model, may launch their drug careers by taking pills from the bottle at the back of the medicine cabinet.

Conclusion

Contrary to stereotypically informed beliefs, social workers can work with drug takers, drug takers can and do change, and the work can be rewarding. Perhaps the most pertinent key for the social worker lies in accepting that drug takers are not significantly different from many other clients in the responses they require; existing skills are readily applicable. A reappraisal of workers' attitudes and expectations will result in more positive outcomes, not just for their interventions with drug takers, but perhaps also for their work as a whole. Social workers are, or should be, involved in the slightly paradoxical business of using their skills and resources to help clients to help themselves, rather than imposing solutions from on high. A delicate balance has to be kept at all times between the specific problems associated with drug use and consideration of the person as a whole, and between a non-judgemental acceptance of the client and the necessity for more directive interventions. Goals should be negotiated with a realistic appreciation of the resources and capabilities of worker and client to achieve them and of the obstacles which may frustrate that achievement. Above all, clients need to be actively involved in the change process and encouraged and confirmed in the belief that change is possible and that they have the ability to carry it through.

Bibliography

AAA (1986), Action on Alcohol Abuse/British Medical Association Professional Division, *Comparative Mortality from Drugs of Addiction*, British Medical Association, London.

ACMD (Advisory Council on the Misuse of Drugs) (1982), *Treatment and Rehabilitation: Report of the Advisory Council on the Misuse of Drugs*, HMSO, London.

ACMD (1984), *Prevention: Report of the Advisory Council on the Misuse of Drugs*, HMSO, London.

Advisory Committee on Alcoholism (1978), *The Pattern and Range of Services for Problem Drinkers*, HMSO, London.

Alexander, B.K. and Hadaway, P.F. (1982), 'Opiate Addiction: The Case for an Adaptive Orientation', *Psychological Bulletin*, Vol. 92, No. 2.

Anderson, H.R. Bloor, K., Macnair, R.S. *et al* (1986), 'Recent trends in mortality associated with the abuse of volatile substances in the UK', *British Medical Journal*, 293, 6 Dec.1986.

Anderson, H.R., Macnair, R.S. and Ramsey, J.D. (1985), 'Deaths from abuse of volatile substances: a national epidemiological study', *British Medical Journal*, 290, 26 Jan.1985.

Auld, J., Dorn, N. and South, N. 'Heroin now: bringing it all back home', *Youth and Policy*, No.9, Summer 1984.

Bandura, A. (1977), 'Self-efficacy: towards a unifying theory of behavioural change', *Psychological Review*, 84, 191-215.

Becker, H.S. (1963), *Outsiders*, Free Press of Glencoe, London.

Bejerot, N. (1972), 'A theory of addiction as an artificially induced drive', *American Journal of Psychiatry*, Vol.128, 842.

Berridge, V. and Edwards, G. (1981), *Opium and the People: Opiate Use in Nineteenth Century England*, Allen Lane/St Martin's Press, London and New York.

Blenheim Project (1982), *How to Stop: A Do-it-yourself Guide to Opiate Withdrawal*, The Blenheim Project, London.

Caplin, S. and Woodward, S. (1986), *Drugwatch: Just Say No*, Corgi, London.

Chein, I. (1969), 'Psychological functions of drug use', in H. Steinberg, *Scientific Basis of Drug Dependence*, Churchill Livingstone, London.

Chein, I., Gerard, D.I., Lee, R.S. and Rosenfeld, E. (1964), *The Road to H: Narcotics, Delinquency and Social Policy*, Basic Books, New York.

Davies, I. and Raistrick, D.R. (1981), *Dealing with Drink*, BBC, London.

DHSS (1984), *Guidelines of Good Clinical Practice in the Treatment of Drug Misuse*, DHSS, London.

Dight, S. (1976), *Scottish Drinking Habits*, HMSO, Edinburgh.

Dole, V.P. and Nyswander, M.E. (1968), 'Methadone maintenance and its implication for theories of narcotic addiction', in A. Wikler, *The Addictive States*, Williams and Wilkins, Baltimore.

Dubble, C, Dun, E., Aldridge, T. and Kearney, P. (1987),'Registering concern for children', *Community Care*, 651, 12 March, 20-2.

Finegan, L.P. (1978),'Management of pregnant drug-dependent women', *Annals of the New York Academy of Sciences*, 311, 135-46.

Glanz, A. and Taylor, C. (1986),'Findings of a national survey of the role of general practitioners in the treatment of opiate misuse', *British Medical Journal*, 293, 16 Aug. 1986.

Gossop, M. (1982), *Living with Drugs*, Temple Smith, London.

Griffiths, R. and Barker, J. (1984), *An Assessment of Drug Problems and Needs in Bermondsey and Rotherhithe*, report of a local working party. Unpublished.

Hartnoll, R. and Grey, G. (1986), *The Drug Situation in Greater London*, Drug Indicators Project, Birkbeck College, London.

Haw, S. (1985), *Drug Problems in Greater Glasgow*, SCODA, London.

Home Office (1986), *Statistics of Drug Addicts Notified to the Home Office, United Kingdom 1985*, Home Office Statistical Bulletin, 40/86, Home Office, London.

Home Office (1986a), *Tackling Drug Misuse: a Summary of the Government's Strategy*, HMSO, London.

Home Office (1986b), *Statistics of the Misuse of Drugs in the United Kingdom 1985*, Home Office Statistical Bulletin, 28/86, Home Office, London.

House of Commons Select Committee on Home Affairs (1985), *Fifth Report from the Home Affairs Committee, Session 1984-5. Misuse of Hard Drugs (Interim Report)*, HMSO, London.

ISDD (Institute for the Study of Drug Dependence) (1981), *Teaching about a Volatile Situation: Suggested Health Education Strategies for Minimizing Casualties Associated with Solvent Sniffing*, ISDD Research and Development Unit, London.

ISDD (1982), *Facts and Feelings about Drugs but Decisions about Situations*, ISDD Research and Development Unit, London.

ISDD (1984), *Drug Abuse Briefing*, Institute for the Study of Drug Dependence, London.

ISDD (1985), *Drug Misuse, a Basic Briefing*, DHSS/HMSO, London.

Jaffe, J.H. (1977),' Factors in the Etiology of Drug Use and Drug Dependence. Two models: opiate use and tobacco use' in A. Schecter, *Rehabilitation Aspects of Drug Dependence*, CRC Press, Cleveland Ohio.

Jamieson, A., Glanz, A. and MacGregor, S (1984), Dealing with Drug Misuse, Tavistock Publications, London.

Laurie, P. (1971), *Drugs: Medical, Psychological and Social Facts*, Penguin Books, Middlesex.

Lindesmith, A.R. (1968), *Addiction and Opiates*. Aldine, Chicago.

MacAndrew, C. and Edgerton, R.B. (1969), *Drunken Comportment: A Social Explaination*, Aldine, Chicago.

Marlatt, A. and George, W. (1984), 'Relapse Prevention: introduction and overview of the model', *British Journal of Addiction*, 79, 261-75.

Miller, W.R. (1983), 'Motivational Interviewing with Problem Drinkers', *Behavioural Psychotherapy*, 11, 147-72.

MRC (1983), *Medical Research Council Annual Report 1982-3*, Medical Research Council, London.

Musto, D. (1973), *The American Disease: Origins of Narcotics Control*, Yale University Press, New Haven, CT.

Parker, H., Bakx, K. and Newcome, R. (1986), *Drug Misuse in Wirral*, University of Liverpool.

Pearson, G., Gilman, M. and McIver, S. (1987), *Young People and Heroin: An Examination of Heroin Use in the North of England*. A report to the Health Education Council, Gower, Aldershot.

Peele, S. (1981), *How Much is Too Much: Healthy Habits or Destructive Addictions*, Prentice Hall, Englewood Cliffs, NJ.

Peele, S. (1985), *The Meaning of Addiction*, Lexington Books, Lexington, Mass.

Peele, S. and Brodsky, A. (1975), *Love and Addiction*, Taplinger, New York.

Preble, E. and Casey, J.J. (1969), 'Taking care of business: the heroin user's life on the street', *The International Journal of the Addictions*, Vol.4, No.1, 1-24, March 1969.

Rado, S. (1933), 'The psychoanalysis of pharmacothymia (drug addiction)' *Psychoanalytical Quarterly*. Vol.2, No.1.

Robertson, J.R., Bucknall, A.B.V., Welsby, P.D. *et al.* (1986), 'Epidemic of AIDS-related virus (HTLV-3/LAV) infection among intravenous drug abusers', in *British Medical Journal*, 292, 527-29.

Robins, L.N., Helzer, J.E. and Davis, D.H. (1975), 'Narcotic use in Southeast Asia and afterward', *Archives of General Psychiatry* 32, 955-61.

Rolleston Committee (1926), *Report of the Departmental Committee on*

Morphine and Heroin Addiction, Ministry of Health, HMSO, London.

Schur, E. (1964), 'Drug addiction under British policy' in H.S. Becker (ed.) *The Other Side,* Free Press, Glencoe, Ill.

SCODA (Standing Conference on Drug Abuse) (1985), *Submission of the Standing Conference on Drug Abuse to the House of Commons Select Committees on Home Affairs and Social Services,* SCODA, London.

SCODA (1986), 'Taking care of the children', *SCODA Newsletter,* Dec./ Jan. 1986/87, Standing Conference on Drug Abuse, London.

Strang, J. and Moran, C. (1985), *The pregnant drug addict.* Unpublished.

TACADE (Teachers Advisory Council on Alcohol and Drug Education) (1984), *Free to Choose,* TACADE, Manchester.

Thorley, A. (1983), 'Problem drinkers and drug takers' in F. N. Watts and D. H. Bennet, *Theory and Practice of Psychiatric Rehabilitation,* John Wiley, London.

Webb, G., Wells, B., Morgan, J. R. *et al.* (1986), 'Epidemic of AIDS-related virus infection among intravenous drug abusers', in *British Medical Journal,* 292, 1202.

Wells, B. (1987), 'NA and the "Minnesota Method" in Britain: time to build bridges', *Druglink,* vol.2, No.1.

Weil, A. (1972), *The Natural Mind,* Houghton Mifflin, Boston, Mass.

WHO (1970), *World Health Organization Expert Committee on Drug Dependence. Eighteenth Report,* WHO Technical Report Series, No.460.

Wikler, A. (1973), 'Dynamics of drug dependence. Implications of a conditioning theory for research and treatment', *Archives of General Psychiatry,* 28, 611.

Williams, A. (1985), 'When the client is pregnant: information for counsellors', *Journal of Substance Abuse Treatment,* Vol.2, 27-34.

Yates, R. (1982), *Sniffing for Pleasure: Guidance Notes on Counselling Young Solvent Users,* Lifeline Project, Manchester.

Young, J. (1971), *The Drugtakers,* MacGibbon & Kee, London.

Zinberg, N.E. (1984), *Drug, Set and Setting: The Basis for Controlled Intoxicant use,* Yale University Press, New Haven, CT.

Zinberg, N.E., Harding, W.M. and Apsler, R. (1978), 'What is drug abuse?', *Journal of Drug Issues,* Vol.8, Winter.

Index